VOLUME ONE

TIDBITS

Treasury of Trivia • A Compendium of Miscellany
Odd & Obscure
Amazing & Amusing
Facts, Stories & Statistics

by J. Spencer
Cartoons by V. Allyn Moravek

JES Press

HELENA • MONTANA

Tidbits Treasury of Trivia & Compendium of Miscellany
Copyright © 1995 by J. Spencer
Illustrations copyright © 1995 by V. Allyn Moravek

Tidbits is a registered trademark of Steele Media. All rights reserved.

Printed in the United States of America. All rights reserved. No part of this book may be reproduced or transmitted in any form or by any means, electronic or mechanical, including photocopying, recording, or by any information storage and retrieval system, without permission in writing from the publisher except in the case of brief quotations embodied in critical articles and reviews. For information address Jes Press at P. O. Box 380, Helena, MT 59624

For rights to reprint individual chapters, contact Jes Press.

Although the author and publisher have researched all sources to ensure the accuracy and completeness of the information contained in this book, we assume no responsibility for errors, inaccuracies, omissions, or any inconsistency herein.

ISSN 1081-0862
ISBN 0-9645583-0-0

J. Spencer
Editor

V. Allyn Moravek
Illustrator

Marty Lord
Cover Design

Expert Printing
Lithographer

Text set in Times

Dedication

To Jerry, who sucked me into the quicksand of Tidbits many years ago— where I've been stuck ever since.

Acknowledgements

This book would not have been possible without the help of the following people: Jerry, for thinking up the entire project in the first place; Dave Steele, for keeping the whole ball rolling; V. Allyn Moravek, for constantly being funny on demand as well as his invaluable advice; the librarians at Lewis & Clark County Library, for their tireless assistance; Marty Lord of Old West Legacy Publications, for graphics and design; Phyllis Cote, Marty Baumann, & Linda Hays, for editorial help; Mom & Dad, for their continued support; the National Forest, for keeping those paychecks coming while I wrote this book; and Glacier Park Inc. for one wonderful winter.

Table of Trivia

Cars	1
Entertainers	7
Random Facts	13
Ants	19
Baseball	25
Money	31
Dreams	37
Language	43
Frogs	49
Kitchen	55
Golf	61
Jewels	67
Hollywood	73
Trivia	79
Ice Cream	85
Names	91
Zany 'Z' Facts	97
Old Age	103
Humor	109
War	115
Presidents	121
Medical Breakthroughs	127
Quick Bits	133
Vitamins	139
Rulers & Royalty	145
Sleep	151

INTRODUCTION

"There is much pleasure to be gained from useless knowledge."
-Bertrand Russell

    The custom of meeting at street corners to engage in idle conversation is an old one. In ancient Greece, it was common to find statues of the god Hermes (messenger of Zeus) or the goddess Hecate (goddess of the sun, moon, and land of the dead) on street corners. This was so people could "worship" as they gabbed. Statues of these two were so plentiful that Hecate became known as Trioditis, which is Greek for "one who is worshipped where three roads meet." In Latin he was known as Trivia, because *tri* means three, and *via* means road or way. Eventually trivia came to mean things of little importance likely to be heard where three roads meet.

    A tidbit is defined as "a choice morsel of food or gossip." In 1987 *Tidbits* was re-defined as a restaurant reader. Each week a newsletter packed with bits of interesting information as well as jokes, quotes, quizzes, cartoons, and advertising was distributed at restaurants all over Helena, Montana by J. Spencer and spouse. It was designed to give people something to do while waiting for their meal— and something to talk about while eating. It provided food for thought. In 1993 *Tidbits* was purchased by Steele Media of Billings, Montana and is successfully expanding nationally. It's distributed not only in restaurants but also in laundromats, doctor's offices, bus stations, waiting rooms, and any other place where people appreciate a few moments of information and entertainment.

    This book contains six months worth of the unedited trivia that has previously been published in the *Tidbits* weekly. New books are scheduled to come out every six months, appearing each January and June. Other books and calendars will be forthcoming. For information on other titles available, contact Jes Press at P.O. Box 380, Helena, MT 59624 or call 1-800-6TIDBIT. For information on how you can become a publisher of your own *Tidbits* weekly, contact Steele Media at P.O Box 35500-22, Billings, MT 59107 or call 1-800-523-3096.

CARS

The First Fact
In 1977 American auto manufacturers recalled more vehicles than they built.

The Auto-Cratic Society
- In 1987, 126,000 cars rolled off assembly lines every working day in the U.S.
- There are now over 400 million cars on the streets of the world, with 125 million of them in the U.S. On the other hand, in 1988 there were only 100 privately owned cars in all of China.
- In 1985, 35% of the world's cars, trucks, and busses were in the U.S.
- 60,000 square miles in the U.S., or 2% of the total land area, is for use by cars. In urban areas, half of all space is set aside for the auto, except in L.A. where it's 66%.
- Each mile of four-lane freeway covers 17 acres of land.
- 15 million acres of land in the U.S. are paved.
- In southern California the average travel speed of 33 m.p.h. is expected to drop to 15 m.p.h. by the year 2000.
- Traffic in New York City averaged 11.5 m.p.h. when horses provided the transportation in 1906. Half a century later, the average speed of auto traffic has dropped to 8.5 m.p.h.
- Transportation consumes 75% of America's rubber supply; 56% of the petroleum; 33% of the steel; 20% of the aluminum; and 27% of the cement. It also accounts for one out of every six jobs.
- Taxpayer subsidies for auto-related items such as police, road maintenance, and medical costs for accidents equals $2,400 per car.
- Americans traveled an estimated 131.7 billion miles on U.S. roads in 1985, averaging 9,534 miles per registered vehicle.
- The average American spends a quarter of their waking hours either driving or working to pay for their car.

The Original Model
The Model T was the first car the common man could own. It was low-priced, reliable, and easy to repair. It could be hitched up to pump water, saw wood, chop silage, or generate electricity. With a change of wheels, it could double as a tractor. It operated as a pick-up truck, hay wagon, taxi, or fire engine. The Model T started out priced at $850, dropping to $360 and later down to $290. Sales rose from 7,000 in 1901 to more than two million in 1925. For three years, half of all cars made in America were Model Ts.

Choice Of Colors
Henry Ford once said that he could give you a car in any color you liked, provided you liked black. The problem was that black paint was the only kind that would go through the spray nozzles easily and dry quickly. Pierre DuPont put his best scientists on the problem. They experimented for months without

success. They worked in laboratories in New Jersey, sharing a floor with other DuPont chemists trying to invent a better celluloid film. In the 1920s movie films had a habit of disintegrating when they got warm. One day the celluloid researchers had just finished mixing a 55-gallon drum of cellulose when the electricity went off and stayed off for three days. The drum of cellulose was left out in the hot sun and forgotten. The celluloid scientists, remembering the mixture later, called the auto paint people over to the drum saying, "Hey, you wanna see 55 gallons of cellulose goo?" The paint scientists were intrigued to see that it had turned into a light brown type of plastic syrup. They figured they'd tried everything else in their paint guns—why not try this, too? It worked. Today you can have a car in any color you like all because the lights went out in New Jersey.

Take The First Left...

In 1903 Dr. Nelson Jackson and his chauffeur Sewall Crocker became the first people to drive coast to coast by car. It took them 63 days. At one point they stopped to ask a woman for directions. Following her instructions, they were surprised when the road came to a dead end in a farmyard, where an old man and woman came out to stare. Retracing their route, they passed the same woman on the road. They stopped to ask why she had steered them wrong. "Oh," she replied, "I wanted Maw and Paw to see you. They've never seen an automobile before!"

History Bits

- The first drunk driving arrest occurred in London in 1897 when taxi driver George Smith was found to be intoxicated.
- The first auto fatality happened in 1896 in London when Bridget Driscoll froze in fear at the sight of an oncoming car, which knocked her down (while traveling at a speed of only 4 m.p.h.) and killed her.
- The first speeding ticket went to Walter Arnold in 1896 for traveling 8 m.p.h. through Wood, England, thus exhibiting "shocking disregard for health and civility."
- The first stolen car was a Peugeot taken from Baron de Zuylen in Paris in 1896. The car was soon recovered in a nearby town. The thief was the Baron's own mechanic.

The All-American Commuter

A typical car with a single passenger gets 30 passenger miles per gallon of gas. So does a full Concorde jet. But the ocean liner Queen Elizabeth II gets only 12 passenger miles per gallon. On the other hand, a 78-seat bus gets 546 passenger miles to the gallon, and a 12-coach diesel train gets 642.

In Europe 40% of the urban population uses public transit systems — busses, railroads, or subways — to get to work. In the U.S. less than 10% do. A car requires nine times more space per passenger than a bus. Nearly one-half of urban commuters drive less than four miles to work, a distance which could be easily covered on bicycle. Only 20% of the miles driven in America are for pleasure such as vacations and visiting. The other 80% is for necessities: work, shopping, etc. Japan, Brazil, and Europe have gas taxes that are up to six times higher than the U.S. average of 30¢ per gallon, explaining why so many people use public transportation in those countries.

From the 1930s through the 1960s, General Motors, Standard Oil, Phillips Petroleum, Firestone Tires, and Mac Truck formed National City Lines which purchased transit systems across the U.S. and then abandoned them as quickly as possible. The aim was to get the American public to depend on cars for transportation, thereby boosting their own business. They were apparently successful in their endeavor. Today 83% of all automobile trips cover less than ten miles.

Accident Facts

- In 1985 a quarter of a million people died worldwide in car accidents.
- More auto accidents happen between 6 p.m. and midnight on Saturday nights than any other time period during the week.
- California has the highest traffic fatality rate, followed by Texas. Rhode Island and Alaska have the fewest fatalities.
- Drivers operate at peak efficiency at 35 m.p.h.
- 75% of car insurance claims contain some element of fraud.
- A man in Sterling, Illinois sued two policemen for $10,000. He unsuccessfully claimed that if they had arrested him for drunk driving five minutes sooner, he never would have had a wreck.
- Only one out of every 2,000 drunk drivers in America is caught and arrested.
- Drunk drivers kill 25,000 people per year, compared to 20,000 killed by homicide in the U.S. annually. They injure more people than criminals who commit assault with a deadly weapon, and cause more property damage than all forgers, burglars, and robbers combined.

Buckle Up

Chances are one in five that you will be involved in an automobile crash this year, according to the Highway Traffic Safety Department. Traffic accidents take twice as many lives as do guns, knives and all other weapons combined. If you are between the ages of 5 and 35, you're more likely to die in a traffic accident than from any other single cause. 75% of highway deaths and injuries occur less than 25 miles from home. 80% of accidents happen in cars that are traveling under 25 m.p.h. Without seatbelts, fatal injuries have occurred at speeds of only 12 m.p.h. A 1968 Swedish study of 28,000 crashes revealed that no deaths had occurred at speeds of up to 60 m.p.h. when lap and shoulder belts were used, except in cases where objects (such as a guardrail) penetrated the car.

Child Car Care

Auto accidents are the number one killer of children over the age of one year old. One out of every 60 children born today will die in an auto accident. Children are much more likely to be killed or injured in accidents than adults, even under identical circumstances. Yet in 1987 less than 5% of children riding in cars were protected with safety restraints. Child restraints could prevent close to 90% of child fatalities and 75% of injuries— *if* they were used. The most common causes of death and injury to children in crashes are being thrown into something, whether a part of the car or another passenger; being crushed by adults who are not belted in; or being thrown from the car. Holding a child on your lap can be extremely dangerous, even if you are wearing a seatbelt. In a 30 m.p.h. collision, a 15-pound child thrown forward has 450 pounds of inertia, hitting the dashboard or windshield with the force equivalent to a fall from a three-story building.

A Court Case

They went on a date. When he dropped her off at her house, she accidentally shut the tail of her coat in the car door. He drove off, dragging her down the street until he heard her cries. She sued him for her injuries, claiming that he was negligent in not checking before he drove off. If you were the judge, would you have held him responsible?

A 1965 Minnesota Supreme Court decided that since she had shut her own coat in the door, she had caused the accident herself.

Rural Roads

People who live in rural areas are 100 times more likely than those living in urban areas to die in an auto accident. The most dangerous place to be on the road is Loving County, Texas, where 91 residents died in auto accidents between 1979 and 1981. That translates to a death rate of 1,465 per 100,000 residents. In Manhattan, however, the rate was only 2.5 per 100,000. The national average is 18.7.

Auto Pollution

A study done by the California Air Quality Management Bureau showed that the air pollution *inside* cars on California's freeways is often higher than the pollution *outside*. They found high levels of benzene, lead, nickel, chromium and manganese in autos traveling the freeway during peak periods. Cars driven with the air conditioning on and the windows closed had even higher pollution levels. The good news is that since lead additives were removed from most gasoline in 1976, the level of lead in our bloodstreams has been dropping. Between 1976 and 1980, blood lead levels were reduced by a third because Americans were no longer breathing lead-impregnated exhaust fumes.

To Strip, Or Not To Strip

As an experiment, two psychologists left a car parked on the street in a middle class residential neighborhood in New York City. They removed the license plates and lifted the hood slightly so it would look as if the car had been stolen or left unattended while its owner went for help. Then they sat back to watch. Ten minutes later, a man with his wife and son took the battery and radiator. 26 hours later, the air cleaner, radio antenna, windshield wipers, chrome stripping, hubcaps, jumper cables, gas can, and left rear tire were gone (the other tires were too worn). The thefts occurred in daylight and the thieves were well-dressed middle class people. The experiment was repeated in a quiet, settled California suburb. This time the car was not touched. The psychologists concluded the anonymity of the big city encourages antisocial behavior.

Babe's Big Ride

In 1921 Babe Ruth was arrested and jailed for driving 42 m.p.h. He was fined $100 and sentenced to spend one day in jail. The jailers let him out early so he could make it to the ball park in time to play in the last six innings of a game.

Chicken Cars

During the oil embargo energy crisis days, an outfit in California called "Captain Calculus and the Normal Street Mechanics Institute" peddled a booklet offering detailed instructions on how to run a car on chicken excreta. It involved heating the stuff to produce methane gas. Entitled *Chicken Doodle*, the book sold for $1.25.

Quick Bits

- In 1986 there were 3,723 Pontiacs in Pontiac, Michigan.
- 2,000 stretch limousines were sold in 1980. 6,500 were sold in 1985.

- 59% of Jeeps sold in 1984 were purchased by people living in urban or suburban areas.
- 18% of Japanese cars sold in America in 1987 were made in America.
- A car theft occurs every 4.6 minutes in America.
- The crash rate for stolen cars is 200 times greater than for normal cars.
- 40% of car theft victims left their keys in the ignition.
- Lightbulbs in traffic lights generally last about 8,000 hours.
- White lines down the middle of the road usually last about four months if they are painted on, or three years if they are coated with thermoplastic applied at 400°F.
- The busiest road in the world is the East L.A. interchange where the Santa Ana, Pomona, Golden State and Santa Monica freeways join. 443,000 cars go by every day.
- The world's biggest parking garage is at O'Hare Airport in Chicago. It is six levels high and can hold over 9,000 cars.
- The city of Chicago hauls away some 55,000 junked cars per year.
- On an average day in New York City, almost a million people use taxis.
- When trucks became popular, railroads lobbied Congress to pass legislation restricting the use of trucks to haul freight. The effort failed in 1930.
- 4% of truckers are women.
- The average car has 15,000 parts.
- In a survey, only 17% of Americans claimed they felt they could trust their auto mechanic.

Slow Down, Dummy

Pisgah, Iowa has a unique speed trap. The town's police chief has taken on a new assistant for the purpose of speed control, but he doesn't get paid a dime. In fact, the new man on the force has to work extra long shifts and doesn't even get dinner breaks. You might say he's a real dummy, and you would be right. The chief placed a dummy made from panty hose stuffed with newspaper in the town's only patrol car, which is parked alongside the highway that runs through town. The dummy (known as Elmer) holds a "radar gun" which is actually an old spotlight. Elmer's affect on passing motorists is astounding. He has also confused some local residents. It seems that one local resident waved at the dummy officer for a number of days before he found out his true identity.

The Final Fact

Of the ten largest corporations in the world, nine of them sell either automobiles or gasoline. The tenth one is IBM.

ENTERTAINERS

The First Fact

In 1980 the Toronto newspaper *Globe and Mail* reviewed a dance program. The show featured a dancer who skipped onto stage carrying a pail, then sat down and urinated into it. The newspaper said of the program that it was a "ho-hum evening" of dance.

Unusual Musicians

- Enrico Caruso and Maria Jeritza starred in a production of the opera *Carmen* in which real horses were used on stage. One nervous horse relieved himself, leaving a huge puddle. When the climactic death scene arrived, Caruso stabbed Maria, but she refused to fall down dead. "Die! Fall, will you!" Caruso shouted. She replied, "I'll die if you can find me a clean place!"
- In 1971 a jazz composer named Roger Kellaway wrote a modern ballet which was mysteriously entitled *PAMTGG*. Audiences soon realized the acronym stood for the TV commercial jingle, "Pan Am Makes the Going Great." The entire ballet was based on airport life, including takeoff, landing, and baggage scramble.
- An opera called *The Prophet,* written in 1849 by Giacomo Meyerbeer, packed houses because of the popularity of the rollerskating scene. Arm in arm, the diva and baritone sang a duet while skating figure 8s around the stage.
- Vladimir Pachmann, an eccentric Russian pianist who died in 1933, enjoyed teasing audiences. A favorite trick of his was to fiddle endlessly with the piano stool before starting to play. He would twist it up, then lower it, adjusting and readjusting it until the audience became impatient. Then he would rush offstage and return with a large book, placing it on the stool. He would settle down, ready to begin the recital when suddenly he'd stand up one more time, rip a single page from the book— and *then* begin to play.

- Louis XI of France asked the Abbot of Baigne to invent an outrageous new musical instrument to entertain his friends. The Abbot, after some thought, borrowed a herd of pigs, ranging from tiny piglets to large boars. Lining them up under a velvet tent, he placed soprano piglets on the right, bass boars on the left, and alto sows in the middle. Next he modified an organ keyboard by attaching each key to a spike that was positioned over the rump of each individual pig. When the Abbot played the keyboard for the royal guests, the spikes pricked the pigs, who each let out a squeal in its own voice range. The tunes were recognizable and the concert was judged a success— though nobody asked the opinion of the pigs.

- The Third Annual New York Avant-Garde Music Festival in 1965 featured a piece called *Prelude in D Minor* by Korean composer Nam June Paik. The piece opened with the demolition of a piano, the amplified cracking of eggs, and the broadcast of a few shrieking feed-back screeches. The second act included nails being driven into an amplified piano and shaving cream being squirted at audience members. In the final movement, a female cellist wearing only cellophane sat upon a stool formed by a man on all fours. Midway through her first piece, she put down her instrument, ascended a ladder, and performed a swan dive into an oil drum filled with water. Then she completed playing the piece. *Prelude in D Minor* got very poor reviews.

Quite An Appetite

Frenchman Michel Lotito is known as "Mr. Eat-All." He makes his living by eating strange things for audiences: razor blades, bottles, knives, beer cans, bolts, knitting needles, and chain. His major accomplishment to date has been consuming a Cessna 150 airplane. At the rate of a few pounds a day, it took him two years to finish the meal. Lotito typically drinks a good deal of mineral oil, cuts the unusual meal into bite-size pieces, and drinks large amounts of water while eating. X-rays have shown that a lot of what he consumes is actually broken down by especially strong digestive juices. The linings of his stomach and intestines are twice as thick as normal. Therefore, he is unable to digest soft items such as bananas and eggs.

Strange Circus Acts

- Annetta Del Mar of Chicago had a really cool act at the 1939 New York World's Fair. Several times a day she would freeze her entire body in ice, except for her head.
- Around the turn of the century, Fred Leslie had a show featuring trained pigs. When one of the pigs got too big to perform his acrobatic act gracefully, Leslie sold it to a farmer who lived next to the circus lot. That night when the pig heard the music heralding the beginning of his act, he used his ladder-climbing talents to scale the fence around his pen. He showed up in the circus tent in time for the act to begin.
- Acrobat Charles Blondin crossed Niagara Falls on a tightrope over 1,000 feet long in 1859. He enlivened the performance by walking part of the way with his hands and feet tied. Next he proceeded on stilts. He then discarded the stilts and walked with his feet in a gunnysack. Finally he took out a small stove and fried up an egg for lunch.

An Incredible Magic Act

A noted magician called for a volunteer from the audience who'd like to be sawed in half. A man stepped forward, and the illusion was very successful. When the volunteer stepped out of the box, he walked back to his seat— where he promptly split in half. His legs walked off in one direction, and his head and torso crawled off in the other. Men screamed and women fainted. The ensuing uproar was so great the trick was never repeated. The magician had developed this trick using twin brothers and a midget. The twins were identical in all respects but one— one of them, named Johnny Eck, had been born without any legs. The fully-developed twin "volunteered" to be sawed in half, but was secretly replaced by his legless twin, dressed only in a suit coat, balancing on the shoulders of a midget who was dressed only in a pair of trousers.

Oddities And Eccentrics

- A Japanese-German inventor named Sadakichi Hartmann offered New York audiences "Odor Orchestras" around the turn of the century. Using many large fans, he would blow clouds of scented smoke into the audience while explaining in broken English that each odor represented a different nation of the world. He had a lot of trouble with hecklers and seldom made it through an entire performance before being booed off the stage.
- Magician Carl Herrmann was entertaining a rich Austrian family in the mid-1800s when he asked to borrow an expensive diamond ring for a trick. He immediately hurled the ring out an open window. Horrified servants rushed to retrieve it. As soon as they went out the door, a parrot flew in the window clutching not only the ring, but also the powdered wigs of the servants.
- Oscar Hammerstein employed a woman named Sober Sue to entertain audiences during intermissions. Her act was to refuse to smile. Hammerstein offered $1,000 to anyone who could make her grin. Comics showered her with their best material. No one knew her facial muscles were paralyzed.

- One of the best-selling records in Italy in 1979 was a disco tune about Pope John Paul II. Some of the lyrics: "He's the groove, he's the man/ the new pope in the Vatican."
- A Soviet machinist named Leonid Germatski trained a choir of sixty songbirds to sing Russian folk songs and waltzes. Led by a blackbird and a nightingale, the bird chorus was extremely popular on Soviet TV.
- Aristotle told the story of the ancient city of Sybaris, where the horses were taught to dance to the music of a pipe. When the Sybarites went to war against the neighboring Crotonians, the Crotonians brought along a lot of pipes. On the battlefield, the pipers began to play, the Sybarian horses began to dance, and the riders were easily slaughtered.

Sword Swallowers Extraordinaire

- John Cummings was an American sailor in 1809. While on shore leave, he and his shipmates watched a magician whose specialty was swallowing knives. The magician was so skilled at sleight of hand that the sailors actually thought he ingested the knives. Wanting to impress his shipmates, Cummings boasted that he too could swallow knives. With a great deal of assistance from booze, Cummings proceeded to swallow his pocket knife, washing it down with more grog. Encouraged by his friends, he swallowed three more knives. Two days later, three of the four knives passed through him naturally, and the fourth one lodged in his stomach with no ill effects. Six years later, while under the influence of alcohol, Cummings was induced to repeat the act. That night he swallowed six small knives, and the next day another eight. He was in considerable pain, but all the knives passed through him within the next month. Later he swallowed four knives, following it the next day with nine more, and the next day four more. This proved to be too much. He lived in a state of extreme pain and emaciation until his death three months later. His autopsy revealed 14 blades still in his intestinal tract, but the immediate cause of death was the backspring of a knife that had lodged in his bowel.
- The French-Canadian sword swallower Cliquot was able to swallow as many as 14 swords to the hilt at once. A skeptical doctor, anxious to show the man as a fraud, grabbed the handles of the 14 blades and yanked them out all at once. It took Cliquot months to recover from the injuries incurred.
- According to one story, a sword swallower named Punkrot Smith became so proficient that he was able to swallow an umbrella. He met an untimely death when the "new-fangled-press-the-button-and-it-flies-up" mechanism deployed accidentally.

Swallowing Pride

- A man who went by the stage name of Mac Norton was a swallower of a different kind. After downing several quarts of water, he would swallow six goldfish and a dozen frogs, then spit them up one at a time, still alive. The ASPCA refused to sanction his act, even though he claimed he never lost a single pet in a career spanning 50 years.

- Nicholas Wood of Kent, England, made his fortune by being able to eat incredible amounts of food. He once reportedly ate an entire sheep and 84 rabbits for one meal. A man named John Dale made a bet with Wood that he could buy two shillings worth of food which Wood would be unable to eat at one sitting. Wood accepted the bet. Dale bought six pots of strong ale and 12 loaves of bread. He soaked the bread in the ale, and Wood began to eat. Soon he became drunk and was overcome by fumes. He fell asleep before finishing the meal. Dale won the bet.
- Egyptian performer Hadji Ali was a remarkable swallower. He would swallow a variety of objects including coins, jewels, and seeds, and then regurgitate the items in the order specified by the audience. For his finalé he drank a quantity of water, followed by a large amount of kerosene. He would spit out the kerosene, spewing it in a long arc over the stage, while an assistant set it on fire with a match. Next he would spout the water, dousing the fire at the opposite end of the stage.

Ghost Story

In 1848 an irritated mother sent her two young daughters upstairs to their room. To get back at her, they repeatedly dropped an apple on the floor to annoy her as she worked in the kitchen below. When she came upstairs to investigate, they claimed they had been talking to a ghost who answered their questions by knocking on the floor. She believed them, bringing the neighbors over to witness the phenomena. The girls quickly learned how to make knocking noises without being detected. Tutored by their older sister (who recognized a potential fortune in the gullibility of people), the two girls learned to crack the knuckles of their toes so loudly it could be heard throughout an auditorium. Margaret and Katherine Fox, ages eight and six, hit the road and appeared on stage all over the world. Members of the audience would ask the girls questions, and the "ghosts" would answer one knock for yes, two for no. Although many investigators discovered their secret, the public refused to believe the act was a fake. The Fox sisters appeared before kings, queens, and czars, earning a fortune over 30 years.

Unusual Shakespeare

- Patients at the Orthodox Jewish Menorah Home and Hospital for the Aged and Infirm in New York staged a facsimile of *Macbeth* in 1964, using modern language. The revised dialog included such lines as the following: Lady Macbeth: "Did I do bad? I wanted my husband to be a somebody." Macbeth: "A king I had to be? A 15-room castle wasn't good enough for you?"
- British playwright Donald Howarth wanted to put on Shakespeare's *Othello* in South Africa. However, employing a black man to play Othello in an otherwise all-white cast violated South Africa's apartheid laws. So he wrote Othello out of the play, creating three new parts for whites instead.
- Orson Welles was starring in a 1956 production of *King Lear* in New York City when he broke his ankle. He played the title role from a wheelchair while his foot healed.

—Entertainers—

The Final Fact

Joseph Pujol was a baker with the unusual ability to expell gas at will and at length. His flatulance was odorless but noisy. With practice he was soon able to "play" songs and do imitations. In the late 1800s he went on tour billed as "Le Petomane" which is French for "The Fart-o-Maniac." He could imitate the expulsions of a bricklayer, a drunk, and a nun. He did impressions of cloth being torn, cannons, and thunder. His animal impressions included a puppy yapping, a dog with its tail caught in the door, a blackbird, a rooster, a duck, a hen laying an egg, a cat, toad, and pig. Using a long rubber tube, he could also blow out a candle, play the flute, and smoke a cigarette. He earned an incredible fortune touring the world with his very unusual act.

RANDOM FACTS

The First Fact

In 1974 a gambler in New York sued his bookmaker for betting losses. He recovered over a quarter of a million dollars on the grounds that gambling was illegal in the state.

Quick Bits about Crime

- Ransom paid for a kidnap victim is tax deductible.
- In federal courts, 71% of people accused of auto theft are convicted and serve an average of three years. However, only 16% of those accused of securities fraud are convicted, and they serve an average sentence of only one year.
- 75% of all murders involve people who know each other.
- In an average 39-hour period, more deaths by handguns occur in America than happen in Britain in an entire year.
- About 75% of all men arrested are under the age of 25.
- The divorce rate for police is higher than any other occupational group in the country at 40%.
- Men are four times more likely to commit an act of violence when angry than are women.

Crime Stories

- In Paris a number of years ago, a film was being made in which an armored car was robbed. Streets were cordoned off and actors and crews worked for days to get the scene down. Several days after the filming had been wrapped up, five bandits held up an armored car and made off with a hundred thousand dollars worth of gold ingots. There were many bystanders witnessing the robbery, but they all thought the film crew had returned to do the scene one last time. Nobody thought it was suspicious, especially since the robbery was taking place just a few yards from police headquarters. If it hadn't been for a nearby off-duty policeman who knew the filming was over, the robbers would have gotten away with it.
- Two young boys in England regularly played near a warehouse where they became friendly with the men who loaded the trucks. The workers would always smile and wave at the boys. One day the boys waved at the men who were loading the truck, but instead of waving back, the men cursed at them before getting in the truck and driving away. Alarmed and concerned, the boys took down the license number and called the police. Acting on this tip, the cops stopped the truck and discovered the men had robbed the warehouse. The stolen goods were recovered, the robbers apprehended, and the boys were thanked in front of the entire school.
- Scotland Yard used to use Labrador retrievers for police work. However, they found that labs don't like to work at night— they prefer to sleep. So they switched to Alsatians instead.

- In naming the horses they use, Scotland Yard chooses names that start with the same letter of the alphabet in any given year. For instance, all horses acquired in a single year may be given names that start with the letter A: Alma, Angela, etc. The next year, all horses will be given names that start with the letter B: Bert, Beverly. This way, it is easy to tell how old a horse is and how long it has been on the force.
- In England during stage coach days, packages would be sent by coach and left at a local inn until their rightful owners came to pick them up. This led to a common scam: a spy would be sent to the inn, where he would surreptitiously write down the names on the packages. Then young kids would be sent to the inn pretending to be errand boys who had been sent to pick up a package for Mister Bates or Mistress White. The innkeeper would hand over the package and it would never be seen again. Because kids were always used in the scam, the practice became known as *kidding*. That's why we now say "you're kidding" when we think someone is not telling the truth.
- Thomas DeVeil was a detective for Scotland Yard. Once he was furiously interviewing a suspected robber. Pretending to give up in exasperation, he quit the questioning and turned to a fellow officer and began a congenial conversation. After talking for some time, he turned to the prisoner and innocently asked if he had a pocket knife he could borrow for a moment. The suspect, taken off guard, offered his pocket knife. DeVeil then brought out the tip of a knife that had broken off in the lock of a place that had been burglarized. The tip fit the end of the broken knife perfectly.

Hunting Facts

- If you refuse to go to heaven if it means you have to leave your shotgun behind, then you might want to contact Jay Knudsen. He heads up Canuck's Sportsman Memorials of Des Moines, Iowa. After you are cremated, his company will load your ashes into shotgun shells and take you hunting. If you prefer, you can have your remains made into fishing lures or duck decoys. Or if you're into a particular sport, the company can even make your ashes into such things as memorial bowling balls or golf clubs. The cost is several thousand dollars, depending on the services required. Off to the Happy Hunting Grounds!
- President Teddy Roosevelt was planning a big-game hunting expedition in Africa when he found out that a famous hunter was in Washington. He invited the man to come to see him in order to give him some hunting tips. After a two-hour meeting the hunter left the President's office. Someone asked, "What did you tell the president?" "My name," replied the hunter. "After that, he did all the talking."

Jokes

- Sign at a ranch gate: "Attention hunters— Please don't shoot anything on my place that isn't moving. It may be my hired hand!"
- Wife to husband: "Couldn't we go fishing instead of hunting? All I have is white wine."

The Best Medicine

Laughter reduces illness and eases pain. It enhances respiration, increases the number of disease-fighting immune cells, brings in oxygen, doubles heart rates, and stimulates internal organs. Bowing to this knowledge, hospitals are installing special rooms made just for laughter. Some nurses are wearing buttons that say "Warning: Humor may be hazardous to your illness" and doctors are writing prescriptions for humor. St. Joseph Hospital in Houston, Texas set up a special "Living Room" which is filled with comfortable couches, easy chairs, stereo equipment, funny videos, art supplies, and a library of humorous books. Patients making use of the room are more relaxed and responsive and make fewer demands on the hospital staff. At UCLA Harbor General Hospital's Children's Ward, Hanna-Barberra set up the Laugh Room with pictures of cartoon characters plastered on the walls and an extensive library of cartoon videos available to young patients all day. At Duke University's Comprehensive Care Center in Durham, North Carolina, the Laughmobile goes up and down the hallways just like the nurse's medication cart.

Fact
One out of every 50 doctors is an imposter.

Misc. Bits

- Researchers theorize that the reason humans may have started to walk upright was because it was cooler. Walking upright reduced contact with the hot desert floor, exposed less skin to direct sunlight, and allowed air to circulate more freely around the body. The loss of heavy fur also reduced the need for water in a desert climate.
- Doctors have long maintained that a baby cannot learn and remember until the age of about nine months, which is about when their language skills start

developing. Recent research challenges this view. In an experiment, babies just three months old have learned that when they kicked their feet, a ribbon connecting their feet to an overhead mobile caused the mobile to move. After learning this, they could remember it two weeks later without having practiced in between. However, researchers found that the entire environment must be exactly duplicated for them to remember the trick. For instance, the babies could not remember how to make the mobile move if a different mobile was used, or if they were placed in an unfamiliar crib or room. Even the pattern of the blanket had to be identical. Researchers theorize that precise visual cues help babies figure out which memory they are supposed to retrieve.

- Jews have tucked written messages to God into Jerusalem's Wailing Wall for centuries. Now Jews from all over the world can have their messages to God delivered to the Wailing Wall even if they are unable to travel to the Holy Land themselves. It's currently possible to fax a message to God. Messages sent to Bezeq, the national telecommunications company in Israel, are taken each evening to the holy site. The company usually receives between 75 and 100 messages per day. They make sure they all reach their destination.

New Inventions

- Alfred Nobel invented dynamite. To ease his conscience concerning all the damage it could do, he set aside money from his dynamite fortune to pay for the Nobel Peace Prize. Nobel also invented plywood and designed some of the first prefabricated houses.
- Bill Malson invented a dehumidifier that not only removes excess moisture from the air, but also catches the extracted water, filters it, chills it, and serves it. The machine can produce three to five gallons a day during optimum conditions of 60% humidity and 80°F. temperatures. It's priced at $2,500.
- Head-up displays have been available in some cars for awhile now. They're electronic displays of speed and other car functions projected on the windshield at driver's eye level. Now researcher Jay Schiffman has come up with a way to project a TV screen onto a windshield in a similar fashion. A projector mounted near the dome light beams the TV image to a mirror lens on the windshield. The matchbook-size picture looks as if it's floating above the horizon just in front of the car. Drivers can only see the picture if they are looking straight ahead. Schiffman feels this is much safer than dashboard-mounted TVs, where drivers have to turn their heads to watch. Schiffman claims that windshield TVs reduce accidents because they prevent the driver from becoming bored. Needless to say, the concept is controversial. Studies are being conducted to see if the accident rate increases or decreases when drivers are watching TV while they go down the road.
- A new technique of organ preservation is being used to keep body parts life-like for use in medical lectures and museum displays. Called plastination, it extracts water from the organ and replaces it with silicon. The organs remain life-like indefinitely.

An Unusual Magazine

The Journal of Irreproducible Results is a science/humor publication. It's devoted to running outrageously unreal studies. Some past articles include: "Lukewarm Fusion", "Survival Strategies Among Animal Crackers", "How Jello Killed the Dinosaurs", and "Dirty Dish Flow Dynamics in a Southern California Kitchen." One article by a Nobel laureate answered the question, "What do you look for when shopping for a lab coat?" There are also reviews of other scientific articles published in magazines such as *Ladies Home Journal* and *Vogue*. Theories propounded in the magazine include: the western hemisphere may sink into the ocean due to the accumulated weight of back issues of *National Geographic* magazines; automotive paint acts as a magnet for shopping carts; and mobile homes attract tornadoes. One scientist wrote an article recommending that erosion in the Grand Canyon could be stopped by filling it with styrofoam packing peanuts. The magazine also gives out an annual Ig Nobel award, named for Ignatius Nobel, a cousin of Alfred Nobel. One year the Ig Nobel Science Education Award was given to Dan Quayle for "Demonstrating, better than anyone else, the need for science education."

Misc. Bits

- 85% of Americans polled said they would rather live in the country than in the city.
- There are 19 nanny schools in America, but only one butler school.

- "In God We Trust" did not become the national motto until 1956.
- In the heyday of streaking, a minister in Pennsylvania posted a sign in front of the church saying, "Streaker, Repant! Your end is in sight!"
- 50% of auto trips taken in the U.S. cover distances of five miles or less.
- There are three firemen on duty at each performance at New York's Lincoln Theater. They are all dressed in tuxedoes.
- The cost of a single Trident missile submarine could cover the cost of operating the United Nations for four years.
- Reykjavik, Iceland, is heated almost entirely by hot springs.
- In Japan cattle are fed shredded newspapers spiked with molasses.

- The average person speaks 450 words in a three minute telephone call.
- In 1970, 16% of women held down two jobs. Now about 38% do.
- In 1950 there was one car for every four people. In 1988 there was one car for every two people.
- 56% of adults eat out at a sit-down restaurant at least once a week. 7% of people eat out almost daily. Men age 18 to 24 and other people age 50 to 64 eat out more often than anyone else.
- There are 23 alligator farms in America.

Yawn Facts

- People watching a test pattern for 30 minutes yawned more often than people watching a 30-minute action-packed video.
- Yawns occur most often the hour after rising and the hour before bed.
- People breathing air with a high carbon dioxide content did not yawn more often than people breathing pure oxygen. This suggests that yawning is not merely a need for increased oxygen.
- People watching a video in which they saw other people *smile* 30 times yawned 21% of the time. People watching a video in which they saw other people *yawn* 30 times yawned 55% of the time. People reading about yawning yawned more often than people reading about hiccups.

The Final Fact

The average human body contains enough fat to make seven bars of soap.

ANTS

The First Fact

In terms of sheer numbers of individuals, ants are among the dominant species on earth.

The Social Order

Ants, which evolved from wasps, are perhaps the most highly developed social insects. There are about 400 different species of ants in the U.S. alone, and about 15,000 species worldwide. The only places that don't have ants are the Arctic and Antarctic. Ants are also unusual because the entire colony consists of females. Males make only brief appearances for mating purposes before dying.

The Dinner Table

Ants are among the most diversified of all insects in the variety of things they eat. Some eat only insects; some eat only plant nectar; some eat only seeds; and some eat only aphid droppings.

Aphids are tiny insects that suck out plant juices for a living. The juices contain more sugar and water than the aphids need, so the surplus is excreted as waste. This sweet excretion is called honeydew. Some ants eat honeydew whenever they happen to run across aphids, but other species of ants actually tend aphids just as humans tend cattle. They take the aphids "out to pasture" on plants during the day, and bring them home to the nest to be "milked" at night. They guard and protect the aphids, driving off insect enemies and building shelters over the aphids as they feed on stems and leaves. They even tend the aphid eggs. Sometimes the wings of the aphids are deliberately cut off to keep them from flying away. When a new queen ant flies off to establish another colony, she will carry in her jaws an egg-bearing female aphid.

Some species of ants will turn members of their colony into living storage tanks of honeydew. Those specialized ants are called repletes. They're chosen when young while they have supple, stretchable skin. After attaching themselves to the ceiling of a storeroom, other ants collect honeydew and pump it into the mouths of the repletes. It bypasses the regular digestive tract and is stored in the abdomen, which stretches to the size of a pea. The replete can regurgitate the honeydew when tapped or stroked by another ant in times of short food supply. In some parts of Mexico, these repletes are collected and are considered a gourmet delicacy.

Some ants cultivate their own food. Leaf-cutter ants carry leaf sections into their nests, chew them into spongy masses, and store them in special chambers where the ventilation and temperature can be regulated. Eventually a fungus garden will grow from the leaf mash, and the ants eat the mushrooms. They collect caterpillar droppings and similar material for fertilizer. These fungus "greenhouses" can be up to 40 inches long, ten inches high, and ten inches wide.

There may be hundreds of such fungus rooms in a colony, and the colony itself may cover an acre. These colonies can contain a half million ants, who are able to defoliate small trees in a single night. When a new queen ant flies off to found another colony, she will carry some of this fungus with her to start a new "garden."

Quick Bit

Tanzanians enjoy a native dessert called white-ant pie. It's made by mixing sweet white ants with banana flour and is said to taste somewhat like honey nougat.

The Homing Instinct

To find food, a typical harvester ant will go straight out from the nest as far as 50 feet, and then start wandering. When it finds food, instead of following the round-about trail back to the nest, it will make a beeline for home, thus refuting the speculation that all ants follow a scent trail. If the soil in front of an ant is scraped away or covered, the ant will continue its direct course home. However, if it is placed inside an enclosure from which it is unable to see surrounding landmarks, it will lose its way until the enclosure is removed. Furthermore, if the ant is picked up and transferred to a new location, it will re-orient itself without hesitation, *unless* it is put down outside the area in which the ants of that colony forage, in which case it will wander about, lost. Ants may use large landmarks as well as the position of the sun to find their way home. If an ant is entrapped in a box in the dark for an hour, when it is released it will strike out again in a direction different from the original direction by an angle equal to the number of degrees the sun has moved during the hour. Some species of ants do leave a scent trail to mark the way *back* to the food. When a forager makes a discovery, it becomes excited and secretes an odorous substance from the abdomen as it returns to the nest. Other ants follow the trail to find the food.

Fast Facts

- One researcher was able to prove conclusively that ants will follow a scent trail to food. The scientist placed food near an anthill and covered the intervening distance with sheets of paper. After the first ant discovered the food and rushed back to the nest, the scientist replaced the original paper with fresh sheets. When the ants swarmed out to get the food, they were unable to find it.
- A single milligram of scent a leaf-cutter ant leaves behind to mark its trail would be enough to lead a column of ants three times around the world.
- Scientist O. A. Battista devised an intelligence test for ants. He put some candy on top of a stool and put the stool in a large tub of water. Then he painted the edge of the tub with slow-drying glue. Six days later, the candy was covered with ants. Using blades of grass and slivers of wood stuck together with saliva, the ants had built a bridge across the water to the stool.
- Another naturalist devised a test that proved that ants can measure, estimate, and communicate. He chopped a grasshopper into three parts: small, medium, and large. He gave each section to a different ant scout from the same

nest. All of the pieces were too big for a single ant to carry. Each ant measured its section with its antennae and then returned to the nest. Would each ant call out the same size crew? Would too many show up to do the work, or too few? The naturalist was surprised to see that 28 ants returned to fetch the small piece; 44 went for the medium piece; and 89 for the large piece. The second crew was twice as big as the first, just as the medium piece was twice as big as the small; and the large crew was twice as big as the medium crew to move a piece that was twice as large.

- When ants find a puddle of fruit juice or a dollop of jelly, they will chew a leaf into a spongy mass and then place it in the middle of the food. When they return later, the leaf has absorbed the juice and the ants carry it home.
- Scientists studying the intelligence of ants have discovered that ants who have learned to pass through a maze when hungry must relearn the same maze from scratch if they enter it when they are not hungry.

Ant Bodies

Ants have two sets of jaws. One set opens side to side instead of up and down in order to grasp food, carry young, fight enemies, build nests, or cut wood. When ants eat, they chew and swallow the food, but the particles pass into a pouch below the mouth where liquid is squeezed out and sent on, while the solids are spit out. They can regurgitate food in order to feed other ants. Larvae eat pre-digested food regurgitated by other ants, and it's considered polite to spit up a droplet of food when meeting nestmates.

Ants have three pairs of legs. Each leg has nine segments and a claw on the end that enables the insect to walk upside-down. Built-in combs on one jaw and each front leg are used to keep antennae and other legs clean. Antennae are used for smell, touch, taste, and hearing. Ants can't recognize anything that is not touched by their antennae. If they walk over the top of an edible seed, they will never know that they missed a meal if they don't touch it with their antennae.

Ants do not have a real heart. The tube that carries blood contracts to force blood forward. They do not have real lungs, either— just tiny openings in their bodies through which oxygen enters and carbon dioxide exits. They don't have true ears, but they have organs on their antennae, legs, trunk, and head that respond to sound vibrations that pass through solid matter. It is not known if they can actually hear sounds that pass through the air. Some ants can make squeaks and buzzes loud enough for people to hear by rubbing a row of ridges on one segment of their abdomen against a hard point on another segment.

About half of all ant species have a sting. Some can inflict a painful bite. Some can squirt poison at their enemies up to two inches away. Some ants have an unpleasant odor, some have an unpleasant taste, and some have spines.

Special nurse ants constantly carry ant larvae from place to place within the nest to keep them at optimum temperature and humidity. Eggs, larvae, and pupae are kept in groups of similar age. They are constantly being licked by nurse ants, which seems to be essential to the well-being of the young. Scientists surmise that the surfaces of the eggs and larvae taste good to the workers.

Ant Nests

Most ants build their nests underground. Some nests may be forty feet long and house ten million ants. Some ants live in trees. Weaver ants build their houses from leaves. To make a nest, workers hold the edges of leaves together while other workers carry silk-spinning ant larvae back and forth across the edges. When squeezed, the larvae are stimulated to produce silk, thus binding the leaves together. Army ants build no permanent home, but are constantly on the move, sometimes in groups numbering 500,000. They are meat eaters and will prey on anything that can't get away from them. One type of army ant is blind and will die if exposed to sunshine. They travel only at night or in deep shade. In some African villages, hordes of army ants are welcomed because they drive out the cockroaches and bedbugs. Whenever they stop, they form an ant bivouac composed of ants who interlock their legs to form a living curtain surrounding the queen and the young.

Quick Bit

In an experiment, a tree limb holding a nest of leaf-cutting ants was placed in the middle of a tub of water. The ants couldn't cross the water and had no way of getting to the ground. But they explored their branch and soon found that one leaf on an outstretched twig hung out beyond the tub and was only two inches above the ground. Many ants gathered on this leaf, and their weight bent the twig even farther. Then one ant grabbed the edge of the leaf with its hind claws and hung down. Another climbed down its body and held on to its head. More ants crawled down and soon formed a chain to the ground. All the others escaped by climbing down this makeshift ladder.

Effective Ant Halloween Costumes

Fast Fact

When establishing a new colony, a winged female destined to become a queen will mate with a male in flight. From that one mating, she will receive and store in a special sack all the sperm she will ever need to fertilize the eggs she will lay in her lifetime.

Some ants can be frozen for long periods of time without harm. Many spend every winter frozen inside logs and stumps. Other ants have survived after spending nine days underwater.

Quick Bit

In a well-established colony, certain members will sometimes decide the group should move to a new location. These pioneers work together to start a second nest, then return to the old home, seize the queen and the young, and carry them to the new place. But other ants in the colony may resist the move. The resisters are picked up and carried bodily to the new nest, but when they are released, they are likely to pick up some pupae and walk back to the old home. They will be hauled back to the new site time and time again, sometimes for weeks until they become discouraged and give in.

Ant Wars

Ants generally treat other species of ants as enemies. Some ant wars consist of simple shoving matches in which no one gets hurt. Other ant wars are bloody and violent. Several nest mates may grab an enemy ant and hold it stretched out while other nest mates literally tear the victim limb from limb. The victors will take over the nest of the defeated, carrying off eggs, larvae, and pupae to be eaten. Other raiding ants, such as the Amazon ants, may invade the nest of another species and carry off the eggs and young in order to raise them as slaves. These slaves find food and feed their masters, who are dependent upon the slaves because their huge jaws, which are so well adapted for fighting, are useless when it comes to eating. They are also unable to dig nests for themselves or to care for their own larvae. There may be six or seven slaves for every Amazon ant. Some tiny ants sneak into the nests of larger species and snitch their food. Sometimes they are tolerated, but when they are no longer welcome, they escape into passages too small for the big ants to enter.

Quick Bit

Scientists have found that aggressive ants, when artificially transplanted as pupae into a colony of timid ants, will grow up timid; likewise, when timid ants are put into a colony of aggressive ants, they will become aggressive.

Quick Bits

- Ants are usually black or brown, but can be red, yellow, green, blue, or purple. Some ant species are an inch long in size.
- Queen ants can live for 20 years. Female worker ants may live as long as ten years. Male ants, however, live only a few weeks. They die immediately after mating.
- One typical Maryland woodland was estimated to contain 1.3 million ants per acre.
- Ants are handy to have around because they eat vast numbers of destructive insects. In the tropics, ants eat more than half of all termites hatched. They also keep the soil loose so rainwater can soak in instead of running off.

The Final Fact

Ant blood is colorless.

BASEBALL

The First Fact

Americans spend twice as much on baseball cards each year as they spend on tickets to major league games.

Antics & Anecdotes

- Casey Stengel once watched teammate L. Cadore catch a small sparrow that was hopping around near the bullpen. Stengel walked over and asked that Cadore give him the bird. Cadore handed the sparrow over, and Stengel stuck it underneath his cap. When he went to bat, some fans cheered while others booed. Stengel simply bowed low, raised his cap— and the bird flew off.
- In 1931 the Boston Braves were losing to the St. Louis Cardinals 12-0. Rabbit Maranville called a time out and gathered the entire team for an infield conference. They gathered in a football-type huddle. Rabbit called the signals, someone snapped the baseball back to him, and the players went crazy tackling each other.
- Bobo Newsom was batting for the Yankees against White Sox pitcher Joe Haynes. He swung and nicked the ball, which rolled back to the pitcher. Realizing it was useless to even try running to first base, Bobo headed back to the dugout. But instead of throwing to first, Haynes just stood and watched Bobo walk away. When the crowd began to laugh, Bobo turned and saw the pitcher still had the ball. So he began to stroll towards first base. So did Haynes. He walked a little faster. Haynes did too. Suddenly he broke into a sprint. Haynes began to run, finally lobbing the ball to first base seconds ahead of Bobo.
- Roberto Gonzalo Ortiz was playing for the Charlotte Hornets in 1941. He was Cuban and with little grasp of English, he had few friends. His closest buddy was a small yellow dog who romped along with Ortiz whenever the team worked out. While the team played, the dog sat patiently in the dugout. During a game one Sunday afternoon, the Charlotte team was up at bat, trailing by a single run. Roberto Ortiz went up to bat. He hit the ball hard, and the crowd leapt to their feet with an excited roar as they watched it soar. The dog, excited by the cheering, saw his master tearing around the bases. As Ortiz reached first base, the dog burst through the clubhouse gate and ran to join Ortiz. Ortiz ran for second as the centerfielder bobbled the ball. With the dog at his side, he went for third, sliding into base, not a moment too soon. The umpire signaled that Ortiz - *and* his dog - were safe! The next day the newspaper added the dog to their account, writing his name, Yellow Dog, under the space usually reserved for pinch hitters and runners: "Yellow Dog ran with Ortiz in the 9th."
- When Dizzy Dean retired as pitcher, made a pretty good sports broadcaster except for his tendency to make up words. Once he commented, "He slud into third" and later said the runner, "slood into second." When he said of one team that "the problem with them boys is they ain't got enough spart" he was asked

exactly what is "spart." He replied, "Spart is pretty much the same as fight or pep or gumption. Like the 'Spart of St. Louis' — that plane Lindbergh flowed to Europe in!"
- Lefty Gomez was called in to see Colonel Jacob Ruppert, owner of the Yankees. Ruppert told Gomez his salary was being cut from $22,000 to $8,000. Gomez responded, "I'll tell you what — you keep the salary, and I'll take the cut!"
- Golf pro Jack Nicklaus once asked baseball pro Hank Aaron what kind of a golfer he was. Aaron replied, "It took me 17 years to get 3,000 hits in baseball. I did it in one afternoon on the golf course."

Unsolicited Advice

- Rabbit Maranville walked over to umpire Bill Finneran after a questionable call and handed him a pair of binoculars. "You'll see pretty good now," said Rabbit.
- Frankie Frisch was managing the Pittsburgh Pirates when a loud-mouthed heckler kept shouting rude instructions concerning how he thought Frisch should be handling the details of the game. Frisch finally went up into the stands and politely asked the man what his name was and where he worked. The heckler was flattered and gave Frisch the information, asking why he wanted to know. "Because," he replied quietly, "I'm going to show up at your office bright and early tomorrow morning to tell you how to run your business."

Quick Bits

- An average of 2.5 baseball gloves can be made from a typical cowhide.
- Only two out of the 161 players in the Baseball Hall of Fame wore glasses on the field.
- Major league teams buy an average of 182 pounds of mud for rubbing baseballs from Burns Bintliff of Delaware each year.
- The market value of Dwight Gooden's rookie-year baseball card was $120 in 1986. In 1987 it was $70.
- The price of an order of sushi at Dodger Stadium is $4.50.

Pitcher Bits

- Rube Waddell was such a great pitcher that all batters feared him. One day the pitcher on the opposing team got a great idea: if he could tire Waddell out before the game, his pitching would be off. So he challenged Waddell to a pitching contest. Whichever one of them could throw the farthest would win $5. Both showed up before the game and threw the ball as far as they could.

Waddell's throw went farthest. The opposing pitcher pretended to be astounded, challenging him to throw that far again. Waddell did. In fact, he repeated the throw about 50 times. Convinced Waddell's arm would be worn out, the rival pitcher handed over the $5 and considered it money well spent. That afternoon during the game, Waddell struck out 14 batters and his team won handily. As he was walking to the clubhouse, he called out to the other pitcher, "Hey, thanks for the workout this morning. That was swell practice!"

- Texas University was up against the Yankees in an exhibition game when Lou Gehrig came up to bat. There were two runners on base with three and two for Gehrig. The catcher signaled the pitcher, the pitcher nodded— then threw a straight ball smack over home plate. Gehrig sent it clear out of the park. The catcher marched up to the pitcher, ranting at him for not paying attention to the signals. "Why did you throw him such a nice pitch?" he yelled. The pitcher was not sorry. "I got to thinking: I'll never pitch a Big League game and maybe I'll never get to see a game at Yankee Stadium, and I sure did want to see Gehrig bust just one!"

- Harvard President Charles Eliot once announced he was thinking of dropping baseball from the curriculum. When asked why, he replied, "I'm told the team did well because one pitcher had a fine curve ball. I understand a curve ball is thrown with a deliberate attempt to deceive. Surely that is *not* an ability we should want to foster at Harvard."

Insults In The Infield

- Bob Fothergill was a big, *big* man. He was a good hitter, but he was very sensitive about his weight. As Leo Durocher got ready to pitch against him, he called out, "Stop the game!" and approached the umpire. When the ump asked what was wrong, Durocher replied, "Don't you know the rules?" he asked, pointing at Fothergill. "*Both* those guys can't bat at the same time!" Fothergill was so angry he couldn't hit well and struck out.

- Restaurant owner Toots Shor was chatting with Alexander Fleming, the man who discovered penicillin. Just then a waiter came over and told Toots that Mel Ott, the Giants' manager, had just arrived. "Excuse me," Shor said to Fleming, "but I gotta go. Somebody important just came in."

Fast Facts

- Lou Gehrig played 2,130 consecutive games.
- Yogi Berra played in more World Series games than anybody else: 14.
- The shortest baseball game was between the New York Giants and the Philadelphia Phillies in 1919. It lasted 51 minutes. The longest was between the San Francisco Giants and the New York Mets in 1964. It lasted over seven hours and had 23 innings.
- When the Philadelphia Phillies went up against the Pittsburgh Pirates on July 10, 1929, a home run was hit in every single inning.
- In a nine inning game against the Chicago White Sox in 1949, the St. Louis Browns used nine different pitchers.

- The spitball was outlawed in 1920, with a clause allowing pitchers already using the spitball to continue until retirement. Burleigh Grimes and his famous spitball lasted another 14 years.
- The Brooklyn Dodgers were originally called the "Trolley-Dodgers" referring to the quick reflexes needed to get out of the way of the trolleys that ran through town.

Goofs And Oops

- Brooklyn had the bases loaded. Hank DeBerry was on third, Dazzy Vance on second, and Chick Fewster on first. Babe Herman came up to bat, hitting a long one to the outfield. DeBerry ran home and scored. Vance advanced to third and decided to stay there. Fewster ran to second and was on his way to third when he saw that Vance had stopped, so he turned around and went back to second. Babe Herman was running full speed ahead, past first, past second, and on to third. At third he made a great slide, only to find Vance already occupying the base. Fewster stood halfway between second and third, wondering what he should do. The third baseman got the ball and began tagging everybody in sight. When the umpire recovered his senses, he called Herman and Fewster out, and Vance safe. It took half an hour for the audience to stop laughing, and it spawned a popular joke: "How's the game going?" "Brooklyn has three men on base!" "Oh really? Which base?"
- Lefty Gomez was up at bat. He swaggered up to the plate, swung a bunch of bats around, tossed them away, then tapped his shoes with his bat to knock out the dirt. On the third tap he hit his ankle by mistake, smacking it so hard he was out of action for two weeks.
- Germany Schaefer was batting against Nick Altrock. There was a man on first. Schaefer swung, missing a fastball. Then the pitcher, pretending he was getting ready to throw to the batter, let loose with a fastball to first base where the

Record for Highest Casualty Toll from a single beanball: 19 June 23, 1967, during a game between the Burgsville Slugs and the Carp City Codfish, when an unfortunate series of events detonated Harvey Simpmeyer, well into his sixty-third chilidog.

runner was leading off. When he got the ball back, Altrock wound up and let fly another fastball scorcher. Schaefer got a second strike. He threw down his bat and walked back to the dugout. "Hey," called the ump, "You've only got two strikes!" "No," replied Schaefer, "It's *three* strikes—I swung at that pitch he threw to first base!"

The New York Mets spent $5,000 on tape to wrap Gary Carter in 1987.

Success Stories

- Chuck had been playing for the Dodgers since 1942. In 1950 he complained to the manager that he either wanted to play more regularly or be traded to a team that would let him play more. He was dismayed when he was traded to the Chicago Cubs, and then to a Pacific League team in L.A. He was a very disappointed player when he started the season in 1952, having pretty much given up on the idea of ever making it into the big leagues. He decided that if he couldn't be a big baseball star, he could at least have fun while playing. One day after hitting a home run, Chuck performed various antics for the crowd. He slid into second, rising with a sweeping bow. At home plate, he vigorously shook the hand of the pitcher, then hammed his way back to the dugout. After the game, a man named Grady came to see Chuck. He said he was a casting director from MGM and offered Chuck $500 a day to do some acting. Chuck got a part as a clean-cut cop, then went back to baseball. Shortly afterwards, Grady called again with another acting job, then another. When his next baseball contract arrived, he decided he had a better future as an actor. He landed jobs in westerns, then was handed the lead roll in the series *The Rifleman*, then starred in *Branded*. Chuck Conners, first baseman, became Chuck Conners, actor.

- Ty Cobb was playing for a semi-professional team in Anniston, Alabama. Even though he was hitting better than ever, the team was so unknown that news of his exploits never made it beyond the local paper. One day Grantland Rice, sports editor of the Atlanta *Journal*, received a postcard in the mail. It said, "Ty Cobb, dashing young star with Anniston, Alabama, is going great guns. He is as fast as a deer and undoubtedly a phenom." It was signed "Mr. Jones." Later another card reached his desk, saying, "Cobb had three hits yesterday, made two sensational catches. Keep your eye on him. Signed, Smith, Brown, Kelly and McIntyre." Another one arrived the next day, "If you're searching for a future star, he's playing here in Anniston. His name is Cobb. He's going to go a long way. Signed, An Interested Fan." Finally, Rice wrote about Cobb in his column, then went to see him play. Thanks to the publicity he got from Rice, Cobb eventually signed with the Detroit Tigers, kicking off a 24-year career in the Big Leagues. Years later, Ty Cobb was being honored at a sports awards banquet. Grantland Rice was seated next to him. When Cobb got up to make his speech, he asked Rice if he remembered getting a lot of postcards concerning what a great young player he was. Rice remembered. Only then did Cobb admit that he himself had sent all those cards to Rice.

Wit Bit

A baseball manager suffering from high blood pressure and ulcers went to see his doctor. The doctor said, "Remember, don't get excited, don't get mad, and above all, forget about baseball when you're off the field." Then he added, "By the way, how could you have let the pitcher bat yesterday with the tying run on second and two out in the ninth?"

The Final Fact

President Richard Nixon opened the 1969 baseball season by dropping the ball.

MONEY

The First Fact

Famous financier John Jacob Aster once said, "A man who has a million dollars is as well off as if he were rich!"

Fast Facts About Fortunes

- A cubic foot of gold weighs 1,204 pounds.
- If someone gave you a million one dollar bills, you would need a box three and a half feet wide, two feet deep, and five feet long to carry it. That's about the size of a coffin.
- If you count 150 one dollar bills per minute and count 16 hours a day, it would take you 20 years to count out a billion dollars.

King Of Misers

- Jack Benny was a wealthy man who became famous for his schtick as a miser. One day he was in a cab when he found he didn't have his wallet with him. He realized he must have dropped it in the hotel bathroom. The cabbie returned him to the hotel. In the bathroom, Benny discovered he did not have a dime to get through the coin-operated bathroom stall. Looking under the door, he saw his wallet on the floor. The only way he could retrieve it was by crawling under the door. Just then another man came in and was convinced that Benny was simply trying to save a dime. Nothing Benny said could convince him otherwise.
- Jack Benny's wife, Mary, was fond of expensive jewelry. One day she was robbed of her favorite piece, an expensive diamond ring. When he heard of the theft, Jack tried to call home, only to be told Mary was out. He tried again and again, until she finally returned home late that afternoon. "Where have you been?" asked Jack. "At the jewelers," she replied, "shopping for another ring." "What! At a time like this you're out shopping for a diamond?" "Sure," she said. "It's like when you fall off a horse. If you don't get right back on, you never ride again!"
- Benny did a charity performance at a benefit and refused any payment. "But just in case I *was* accepting money, how much was I refusing?" he asked.

Some That Got It...

- Bing Crosby was asked by an interviewer how he managed to maintain such a calm, unruffled appearance. Crosby pulled a big wad of bills out of his pocket, waved it at the interviewer, and said, "This helps!"
- A magazine editor wrote to oil magnate J. Paul Getty asking him to write an article for them describing why he was so successful. A check for a sizeable sum was enclosed. Getty cashed the check and returned his "article" which was composed of two sentences: "Some people find oil. Others don't."
- When a reporter asked Getty if it was true he was worth over a billion dollars, Getty said, "Yes, but remember, a billion dollars doesn't go as far as it used to!"

—Money—

- Nubar Gulbenkian was a rich industrialist who indulged in all the things money could buy. One day he brought home the latest in expensive cars. "It's got disk brakes, whatever they are," he announced. "And it has an automatic transmission, whatever that is. It has power steering, whatever that is. And it can turn on a dime, whatever *that* is!"
- While filling out a market research form, Gulbenkian found a spot that asked "Position in life." He filled in "Enviable."
- William Vanderbilt, son of railroad magnate Cornelius Vanderbilt, had a fortune that was worth an estimated $200,000,000 shortly before his death in 1885. He remarked, "I have had no real gratification or enjoyment of any sort more than my neighbor on the next block who is worth only half a million."
- John Spencer-Churchill, 10th Duke of Marlborough, lived in Blenheim Palace in splendor. Once he spent the night with his daughter, who lived under considerably more modest circumstances. In the morning she was surprised to hear him bellowing down the hallway that his toothbrush was not working properly. When she investigated, she found him upset because his toothbrush was failing to foam. She explained to her wealthy father that a toothbrush did not foam unless a toothpaste or powder was applied to it first— a task which the Duke's valet performed for him every morning.

Some That Don't

- Writer Alexander Woollcott once toured the fancy mansion and grounds of wealthy playwright Moss Hart. He said, "That's just what God would have done— if he had the money."
- While campaigning in 1960, J. F. Kennedy visited a mine in West Virginia. "Is it true you're the son of one of our wealthiest men?" asked a miner. Kennedy admitted he was. "Is it true you've never wanted for anything and had

everything you wanted?" "I guess so," he said. "Is it true you've never done a day's work with your hands all your life?" Kennedy nodded. "Well, let me tell you this," said the miner. "You haven't missed a thing!"
- Italian composer Rossini was old, famous, and respected— but far from wealthy. Many of his fans chipped in and raised 20,000 francs in order to raise a statue in his honor. "Give me the 20,000," said Rossini, "and I'll stand on the pedestal myself!"
- Naturalist John Muir remarked that he was richer than millionaire magnate E. H. Harriman declaring, "I have all the money I want and he hasn't!"
- Thales was a Greek philosopher. People often taunted him, saying, "If he's so smart, why isn't he rich?" Thales used his knowledge of meteorology to predict an upcoming bumper crop of olives. He bought all the olive presses he could possibly find. When the olive crop came in, he rented the presses for high rates and made a fortune. Having proved his point, he sold the presses and returned to his philosophical pursuits.
- Abe Lincoln received a letter from a New York firm requesting information concerning the financial condition of a neighbor. Lincoln replied, "First of all, he has a wife and baby; together, they ought to be worth $50,000 to any man. Secondly, he has an office in which there is a table worth $1.50 and three chairs worth $1.00. Last of all, there is in one corner a large rat-hole, which will bear looking into. Respectfully yours, A. Lincoln."

Quick Bits About Cash
- The word 'cash' comes from the Chinese word *kase* meaning small coin. 'Money' comes from the Roman goddess Juno Moneta, who stood guard over the temple where coins were minted.
- Coins could once be cut into pieces to make change. A Spanish dollar could be divided into eight pieces. That's why pirates had pieces of eight; American slang got two bits; and England ended up with the halfpenny and the farthing, which was originally a 'fourthings' or a fourth of a penny.
- The one-rupee note of India has its value written out in 13 different dialects.
- The first coin bearing the name *United States of America* was minted in 1787. It was worth a single cent and bore the slogan "Mind Your Business."
- When the first U.S. mint opened, individual citizens could take their gold and silver there to have it made into coins, free of charge.
- The most valuable U.S. coin is the $3 gold piece minted in 1870. Only one is known to exist.
- All coins currently minted bear a presidential portrait. By law no living person is allowed to be portrayed on money of the U.S.
- There are only six denominations of paper money in use today in the U.S.: $1, $5, $10, $20, $50, and $100.
- A typical dollar bill lasts about a year and a half in circulation.
- A damaged bill that is still three-fifths intact can be redeemed for full face value. If only two-fifths are left, it can be redeemed for half face value. If less

than that remains, it's worthless.
- If an asterisk appears in front of the serial number on a bill, it means it's a replacement for the original, which was defective.
- About $200 billion in coins and bills is in circulation in the U.S.
- Only 20% of money transactions and payments are made with coins or cash. The rest are done by check or credit card.
- The first credit card in America was introduced in 1959.
- In Nevada you can post bail with a credit card.
- Today the U.S. mint produces about 13 billion coins annually. 39 million pennies are minted every day. That's enough to fill 210 wheelbarrows.

Giving It Away

- James Gordon Bennett was an eccentric newspaper owner and millionaire. His self-proclaimed purpose in life was to get rid of all his money. He once tipped a night guard on a train an incredible $14,000. The guard stepped off the train, resigned his job, and opened a restaurant. Another time he went to his favorite restaurant for his favorite meal but found his favorite table occupied by people who were only halfway through their meal. He immediately offered the owner of the restaurant $40,000 to purchase the entire business. The owner agreed. Bennett then went over to the diners, explained that the restaurant was under new management, and ordered them to abandon their meal and leave. He then ate his meal at his customary table. When he left, he gave the owner of the restaurant a nice tip— he gave the restaurant back. Once while he was interviewing a job applicant, he squirmed uncomfortably in his chair. Finally he reached into his back pocket and pulled out a wad of bills that had been making it hard for him to sit. He hurled the money into the fire. The man he had been interviewing sprang up and pulled the money out of the flames. "Give the money to me," said Bennett. He then promptly threw the bills back into the fire. "That's where I want them to be!"
- Millionaire J. P. Morgan was asked to contribute to the founding of an Ivy

League medical school. When representatives came to see him, Morgan said he was in a hurry and asked them to quickly show him the proposed plans of the campus. When they laid out the plans, Morgan said, "I'll give that, that, and that," pointing out three buildings. He then rushed from the room before he could be thanked.

Keeping It For Yourself

- John D. Rockefeller, Jr. made a collect call from a pay telephone which refused to return his quarter. He called the operator, who dutifully requested his name and address so the phone company could mail a reimbursement. "My name is John D....Oh, forget it— you wouldn't believe me anyway."
- Financier Sir Nathan Rothschild hired a cab one evening and gave the driver a modest tip. The driver complained, saying, "Your son always tips me a good deal more than this!" Rothschild replied, "I daresay he does! But then, you see, he has got a rich father. I haven't."

Counterfeiting

- Indians living on the coast of the U.S. used shell money called wampum. In 1760 a man named Campbell set up a factory to mass produce wampum in what is now Hackensack, New Jersey. Because of this, wampum was rapidly devalued and was soon abandoned by the Indians.
- About one-third of the money in circulation in Civil War days was counterfeit. Lincoln ordered a permanent force set up to deal with the problem. That force became the Secret Service. At one point they were so diligent that they prevented a baker in Philadelphia from baking cookies that looked like pennies.
- Charles IX of France was a good counterfeiter. He flooded the country with fake money to force the enemy's economy to collapse.
- The Chinese used to make fake paper money which they called hell money. It was burned with corpses in order to give the deceased something to spend in the next world.

Fast Fact

When Nitocris, Queen of Babylon, died, she had this inscription put on her tomb: "If any king of Babylon after me should be short of money, he may open this tomb and take as much as he wants, but only if he really is in need of it." King Darius I thought it was a shame that the riches should go to waste inside a tomb, so he ordered the tomb opened even though he did not need any money. Inside he found no money at all, only a note beside the Queen's body saying, "If you had not been greedy of gold and fond of base gain, you would not have thought of ransacking the graves of the departed."

Queen's Valentine

Valentine Dale was on a diplomatic mission to Flanders on behalf of Queen Elizabeth I when he ran short of money. He had to write to the Queen to ask for an advance, which he dreaded. The Queen was notoriously stingy and he wondered what he would do if she refused. He sat down and wrote two letters.

The first was to the Queen in which he stated in a businesslike tone the progress of his mission and the reasons he needed more money. The second letter was to his wife in which he described in glowing terms the success of his mission, how much he missed her, and how he hoped to be home soon. He also mentioned his dire lack of cash. When the letters were mailed, the letter to the Queen was addressed to his wife, and the letter to his wife was addressed to the Queen. Queen Elizabeth was amused to find herself reading a letter full of terms like "sweetheart" and "darling." The mix-up tickled her funny bone and she sent the money he needed without delay. She never knew he had mixed up the letters on purpose for this reason.

Quick Bit

The Bank of England lost so much money to highway robbers that when they were shipping bills to branch offices they began to cut them in half and send only one half at a time.

The Final Fact

Ross Perot lost $450 million on the stock market on April 22, 1970.

DREAMS

The First Fact

In an experiment, monkeys were strapped into chairs in front of a video screen and taught that they must repeatedly press a bar in front of them whenever a certain image appeared on the screen. If they didn't, they would receive a shock. After several days of intense training which included sleep deprivation, the monkeys were allowed to fall asleep, still strapped to the chair, while their sleep was monitored. Not long after entering the REM dream stage, the animals began rapidly pressing the bar in front of them as they dreamed about the video screen.

Dreaming Up An Answer

- Making lead shot for shotguns was a difficult and time-consuming process in the 1800s. Lead was rolled into sheets and the sheets were chopped into bits, or it was drawn into wire and cut into pieces. The resulting shot was expensive and of poor quality. James Watt, inventor of the first practical steam engine, had a recurring dream one week. In it, he seemed to be in a heavy rainstorm but instead of water drops, he was being pelted with tiny lead pellets that rolled around on the ground. Intrigued by the dream, Watt experimented by dropping molten lead from the top of a church tower into a water-filled moat. When he recovered the pellets he found that they were perfectly round. To this day, lead shot is made by the process Watt dreamed up.
- Elias Howe was trying to invent a sewing machine, but he was having a major problem. He couldn't figure out where to locate the eye of the needle. The eye of a standard needle is located in the end of the needle furthest from the point, but machines incorporating this traditional design failed to work. He was at wits end and rapidly running out of money when he fell asleep one night and had a strange dream. In the dream he was being led to his execution. The king had ordered him killed because he could not design a sewing machine. He was surrounded by guards who were all armed with spears that were pierced at the head. When Howe awoke, he realized this was the solution to the problem. In short order he had designed a sewing machine whose needle had the eye at the head.
- Robert Louis Stevenson wrote a story called *The Traveling Companion* and sent it to an editor. The editor rejected the story saying, "This is an ingenious piece of work but your plot is very weak." Stevenson realized the criticism was true but he was at a loss to figure out how to improve the tale. Then one night he re-read the story before falling asleep. In a dream, he saw his story being acted out with a different plot twist. When he awoke, he wrote down the details of the dream and then reworked the story. The result was *Dr. Jekyll and Mr. Hyde*.
- Joseph Mandemant was a top anthropologist. One night he dreamed he was looking at a what he recognized as a particular cave in France. He saw cave men

around a fire and, above them in the flickering light, drawings on the cavern's roof. Then two of the cave people went to a different part of the cave. In the dream, Mandemant saw the roof collapse, sealing the two inside. Then he awoke. He wrote down the details of the dream. Shortly afterwards he had the opportunity to go to the cave he had seen while sleeping. By tapping with his hammer, he was able to hear hollow echoes, meaning that there was a previously undiscovered chamber behind a slab of roof that had caved in. Workmen drilled through the rock wall and there they found a secret chamber just as Mandemant had predicted. Although no human remains were discovered, the pictographs were found on the ceiling.

- Wallis Budge had a passion for hieroglyphs. He wanted to go to college to study ancient languages, but he was too poor to afford tuition. Luckily, he was invited to participate in a competition involving ancient oriental languages. The winner would receive a scholarship. This was his big chance, and he began to cram for the test. He knew only that there would be four questions on the test, but he did not know what languages or subjects they would cover. The night before the competition was to be held, Budge had a dream. He saw himself being taken to a small shed and handed several strips of green paper. He was asked to translate the texts written on the paper. He looked at the sheets and saw the text was written in cuneiform Assyrian characters and in the Akkadian language. He experienced a sudden feeling of fright because he did not know these languages well — and then he woke up. When he fell back to sleep, he dreamed the same thing a second time. He could not get back to sleep, so he got up and found a book that explained these two ancient languages. He spent the night studying them. When he arrived for the exam the next day, there was not enough room for him in the crowded hall. He was taken to a shed instead. There he was handed four slips of green paper as the exam master explained he used green paper because it was easier on his eyes. On the paper were the identical texts he had seen in his dreams. Budge won the scholarship because of his dream. He went on to become one of the world's foremost authorities an ancient languages. He is best remembered for translating the *Book of the Dead*.

Dreams Come True

- In England in 1812, a wealthy man named John Williams dreamed three times that he was in the House of Commons when he saw a man in a dark green coat with shiny buttons walk up to Prime Minister Spencer Perceval and shoot him. The dream disturbed him so much that he told his wife and friends about it, asking them if they thought he should send a warning to Perceval. The consensus was that Perceval would think him a crackpot if he did so. One week later, Spencer Perceval himself woke up and told his family that he had dreamed that a man wearing a dark green coat with shiny brass buttons had walked up to him in the House of Commons and shot him. His family begged him to pay heed to the warning in the dream, but Perceval shrugged it off as 'just a dream' and went to work anyway. He was shot to death as he walked through the lobby

of the House of Commons by a man wearing a green coat with brass buttons.
- It was gold rush days in 1864 and Lloyd Magruder was traveling with several companions across a remote mountain pass in Idaho, carrying about $35,000 worth of gold. Late one night three men in the party attacked the other five men, killing them with an ax. Lloyd Magruder never knew what hit him. After taking the gold and several mules, the three criminals threw the bodies of their victims into a canyon and headed for town. But back in Lewiston, Idaho, Lloyd Magruder's closest friend, Hill Beachy, was asleep and dreaming. In his dream he saw Lloyd being killed by an ax. He saw the killer's face clearly. The dream was so vivid, he told his friends about it the next day. Meanwhile, the killers found that they were unable to get their pack animals across the swollen Clearwater River. They left the animals with a rancher until the river went down, then headed into town. When they arrived there, Hill Beachy recognized the face of the man he had seen in his dream. Instantly suspicious, he did additional investigation and found they had left their pack animals with a rancher. A little checking revealed that those animals belonged to Lloyd Magruder. Furthermore, Lloyd's saddle, personal belongings, and gun were found with the animals — but Lloyd was missing. An arrest warrant was issued for the three men, who fled. Hill Beachy tracked them to San Francisco. There the three were arrested, tried, found guilty, and hung on the gallows— because Hill Beachy believed in his dreams.

- In the spring of 1912 the minister of the Rosedale Methodist Church in Winnipeg took a little nap before church. He dreamed a nightmare in which he saw waves and water and heard people screaming and shouting. Then he heard them singing an old hymn, "Hear, Father, while we pray to Thee for those in peril on the sea." He was so disturbed by this dream that at the close of his sermon, he told the congregation of the dream and requested that they all stand and sing the song he heard in his dream. The next day's newspapers carried the

news that the *Titanic* had gone down at the same time the minister was having his dream.
- World War I was in full swing. Bobbie Bereford was four years old when he laid down for a nap on October 11, 1918. He began talking in his sleep, "Poor Mrs. Timms! Won't somebody tell her? Edwin is dead! Dead in the mud!" His parents were baffled. The family doctor happened to be passing by so they called him in to hear their son's strange exclamations. When the boy awoke, he remembered nothing of the dream. Neither Bobbie nor his parents or the doctor knew of anyone named Mrs. Timms, but the doctor's wife recalled later that day that there was a Mrs. Timms living about 20 miles away. When they investigated, they found that she had a son named Edwin who was away at war. A few days later a telegram confirmed what little Bobbie had dreamed. Edwin had died the day before Bobbie had his strange dream.
- Rudyard Kipling had a dream in which he saw himself at a formal function in a big hall with rough stone flooring. There was a crowd of people around him and his view was obstructed by a fat man in front of him. A man touched him on the sleeve and asked, "May I have a word with you?" Then he awoke. It was six weeks later when this dream was fulfilled down to the last detail when Kipling attended an official gathering. Although the man who wanted to speak to him had nothing consequential to say, Kipling was amazed at the dream's fulfillment.
- In 1937 Lt. Colonel Dickson was the British political agent who was ruling Kuwait. He had a dream one night in which he saw the location of a huge oil field and the spot where a drill could tap into it. Acting on the dream, he managed to overcome the scepticism of his superiors and ordered a drilling team to put in a well at the spot he had dreamed of. In 1938 they struck oil, and as a result, Kuwait became the country with the highest per capita income in the world.

Sweet Dreams

- About a quarter of the time you spend asleep is spent dreaming.
- A typical person has an average of 1,460 dreams per year.
- The average adult has around one nightmare per year.
- Nonsmokers dream more than smokers.
- Young people dream more than older people.
- Women dream more than men.
- Intelligent people dream more than less intelligent people.

Follow Your Dreams

James Chaffin was an eccentric North Carolina farmer. He had four sons, but favored his son Marshall above the others. In a will he made out in 1905, he left everything he had to Marshall and nothing to his wife or other sons. He showed everyone the will and made them understand this was the way he wanted it when he died. It caused some hard feelings, but his family was accustomed to his peculiarities and accepted his desires. When he died in 1921, Marshall got

—Dreams—

everything. Family relationships were strained because of this. Four years later, James Chaffin Junior, the second son, dreamed that his father appeared beside his bed, wearing his favorite old overcoat. He slowly pulled back the coat and pointed to the inside pocket on the left breast. James awoke and related the dream to his wife and then to his mother. His mother recalled the old coat and remembered that she had given it to the eldest son, John. Together they traveled to John's house and found the coat in the attic. When they looked at it, they found a pocket on the inside left breast, but it had been sewn shut. Slitting the stitches, they found a piece of paper that said, "Read the 27th Chapter of Genesis in my daddy's old Bible." It was written in James Chaffin's handwriting. Collecting some witnesses, they returned to the mother's house where she located the old Bible. When they tried to open it to the 20th chapter, they found that two pages had been folded to form a pocket. Inside was a slip of paper reading, "After reading the 27th Chapter of Genesis, I, James Chaffin, do make my last will and testament...I want my property to be equally divided between my four children, if they are living at my death...Written this day January 16, 1919." The 27th chapter of Genesis told of how the younger brother, Jacob, had won his father's favor and had cheated his older brother, Esau, out of his birthright. Marshall had died in the meantime, but his wife conceded that the will was authentic. The property was redivided, more equally this time, because of a dream.

Corporal Teddy Watson was killed at Dunkirk in 1940. His mother was especially distressed because she did not know where he was buried. More than anything she wanted to find her son's final resting place. In a dream, she saw a military cemetery with hundreds of white crosses in rows. At the corner of the cemetery she saw her son, who smiled and then disappeared. In the dream she saw landmarks by which she could identify her son's grave. Soon after the dream, Mrs. Watson traveled to the military cemetery at Dunkirk. There she found everything exactly as it had been in her

dream. She indicated a grave to the officer accompanying her and asked that the remains be exhumed. When the grave was opened, the rosary, monogrammed cigarette holder, and picture in a locket were found to be those of her son.

Max Hoffman was five years old in 1865 when he contracted cholera. The doctor, finding no pulse or signs of life, pronounced him dead. Young Max was buried. But the next night his mother dreamed she saw him struggling to escape from his coffin. She saw his hands clasped underneath his right cheek. She insisted the grave be opened, but her husband dismissed the dream as the overreaction of a distraught mother. When she had the same dream the next night, she would not take 'no' for an answer. In the middle of the night the grave was opened. In the coffin they found the boy just as was predicted in the dream, with his hands clasped under his right cheek. The comatose boy was rushed to the doctor, where he was revived. Max Hoffman lived into his 80s, cherishing the little metal handles of the coffin in which he was buried.

Fact

Scientists at the Sleep Disorders Center in New York have found that some people are not only sleepwalkers— they are also sleepeaters. Such people are typically obsessed with food or dieting while awake. When they're asleep, their compulsions take over and lead them into the kitchen. While sleeping, such people will eat great quantities of various foods, putting together strange combinations and often eating foods raw. And they never clean up after themselves.

The Final Fact

Once Betty Ford heard Gerald Ford talking in his sleep, saying "Thank you, thank you, thank you." When she woke him up, he said he had been dreaming that he was in a receiving line, shaking hands with a long line of people.

LANGUAGE

The First Fact
The Roman word for secretary meant 'one who keeps a secret.'

Phrase Facts
- Special holidays were originally marked on the calendars using red ink. These are now called 'red letter days.'
- If you stick with someone 'through thick and thin,' you're riding with them through the difficult thickets and the easy woods where the trees are thin.
- Back in medieval days, most towns were inside gated fortresses. When the king trusted an especially good friend, he would be given 'the keys to the city.'
- When wool is dyed before it is spun into yarn, it keeps its color much longer. Thus, the expression 'dyed in the wool.'
- A small spot behind the ears of newborn animals is the last spot on the hide to dry after birth. Anyone who is still 'wet behind the ears' hasn't had a chance to experience much yet.
- In the 1500s the French played a game similar to backgammon that was called *lourche*. The player who was falling behind in the game was 'left in the lourche,' today known as being 'left in the lurch.'
- During the Revolutionary War, when soldiers said, 'lock, stock, and barrel' they were referring to an entire gun.
- In the first century B.C. the Parthians conquered many nations by using a new battle ploy. They would turn away from the enemy, feigning defeat. But as they fled, they would turn around and shoot arrows at their pursuers. The maneuver was called a 'Parthian shot' which today is known as a 'parting shot.'
- Hounds are used to hunt raccoons and chase them up trees. It's a very stupid hound indeed who goes around 'barking up the wrong tree.'
- In the 1600s when craftsmen finished making a pitcher, they filled it with water to see if it held water. Nowadays we speak of an idea that 'doesn't hold water.'
- When folks want to hide the fact that they're laughing, they cover their mouth with their arm, resulting in 'laughing up their sleeves.'
- In sports, the beginning line of a race was scratched into the dirt and thus became known as scratch. When you make something 'from scratch,' you are starting at the very beginning. Likewise when you 'toe the mark,' you have your foot against the scratch mark and are ready to start the race.
- Is your house as 'clean as a whistle?' A whistle must be clean and dry inside to produce a clear tone.
- When a chicken is placed on a butchering block, it will naturally stick its neck out, making it easier for the butcher to decapitate it. Therefore it's pretty dangerous to go around 'sticking your neck out.'
- At harness races held at local county fairs, the horses were sometimes over-eager to start the race and would often break ranks and head down the track before the race began. It was important that the riders be able to keep their

horses under control— thus the phrase 'hold your horses.'
- Witches on secret errands for the devil would depart from their homes on broomsticks after dark so they wouldn't be detected. This gave us the expression 'fly-by-night.'
- In some parts of England, *dander* meant anger, so 'to get your dander up' was literally to become angry.
- A century ago shirts were not as well made as they are today, and a nice looking shirt would tend to restrict the movement of the arms. Therefore when a fist fight was imminent, the first order of business was to remove the shirt to have better swinging power. Today when someone gets antsy, we tell them to 'keep your shirt on.'
- Often the mustard on the market was of very poor quality or had been adulterated. This led to the phrase 'to be the proper mustard' which has evolved into 'it doesn't cut the mustard.'
- Some Indian tribes had a ritual where, when peace was declared between two tribes, they would ceremoniously 'bury the hatchet.'
- In the 1500s one's property boundary would be indicated by a line cut by a plowshare across the field. Now that's where we 'draw the line.'
- Beasts of burden and other animals have historically been led about by means of a ring in the nose to which a leash is attached; hence the phrase 'lead by the nose.'
- In days of old, expensive carpets were put on the floors in rooms where the gentry resided. Generally the only time a subservient person would get to walk on a carpet was when they were being 'called on the carpet' to be reprimanded in front of their wealthy employer.
- In the 1600s there was a drinking game called High Jinks. Dice were thrown and the high roller was required to spend the rest of the evening in the character of some chosen figure, either real or historical. If at any time he broke character, he was required to take a drink. In another version of the game, the person would have to repeat a nonsense verse a certain number of times, taking a drink

One day at the place now known as Quicksand Flats:

each time the tongue slipped. The more drinks, the more slips of the tongue. Today, 'high jinks' are pranks or frolics.
- When rivers were the highways, each spring townfolk would have to go out and break the ice on the water so that boats could easily pass. Now 'breaking the ice' makes it easy for conversation to occur.
- In cock fights, a rooster which has an artificial spur attached to its heel for battle is said to be 'well-heeled.' When people armed themselves before entering a dangerous place, they were also said to be well-heeled. Now, perhaps because money can make many dangers disappear, any wealthy person is well-heeled.
- The two ventricles of the human heart resemble the two valves of a mollusk known as a cockle; thus, something pleasing 'warms the cockles of our hearts.'
- When we clear our throats politely it is called a 'hem' as in 'ahem.' When we clear our throats more vigorously with a choking effort, it's called a 'haw.' When we can say nothing and only manage to clear our throats, we are 'hemming and hawing.'
- In the days of knights in shining armor, some knights would go from town to town offering themselves and their lances for hire to the highest bidder— the first 'freelancers.'

Quick Bits

- Dice were invented by the Arabs. They called a single die *al zahr* which became *hasard* in French before it became our hazard.
- A Ouija board comes from the French word for yes *oui* and the German word for yes *ja*.
- 'Bonfire' was originally a 'bone fire' or funeral pyre.
- The Lapland word for deer is *rein*, so the word 'reindeer' is actually redundant.
- Gospel came from the words 'God spell' meaning good tidings.
- *Infans* is Latin for 'not able to speak,' meaning a baby, or a member of the infantry, who is not allowed to speak unless spoken to.
- Ancient Romans were very superstitious— so much so that the wealthier ones employed a servant whose sole purpose was to make sure the master entered the house with the proper foot first, lest bad luck befall him. That servant was of course called the 'footman.'
- In ancient France the town bell would ring each night, signaling the citizens to *couvre-feu* meaning cover fires, and go to bed. Today we call it a 'curfew.'
- The Greeks named the lion *leon* and they named the tiger *pardos*. But when they encountered a new animal, they didn't know what to call it so they named it the lion-tiger: 'leopard.'
- Auction comes from the Latin word for increase.
- *Bursa* is the Latin word for pocket, which helps explain why disburse means 'out of pocket' and reimburse means 'back in the pocket.' Bursitis is the

inflammation of the pockets which joints fit into.
- The word 'bureau' originally meant a wool cloth that was placed on top of a writing desk. Then it became the desk itself. Next it denoted the room where the desk was located, and now it means an entire governmental division.
- *Thrillen* was the middle English word for pierce, and today 'thrill' means to pierce the heart or emotions.
- The Greek word for ship was *naus* and because so many people get seasick, we now have the word 'nausea.'
- The word tax comes from the Latin word meaning 'touch sharply.'
- An ancient Greek physician found little tubes running all over the body and assumed they carried air to the tissues. He named them *arteria* meaning windpipe and today they are called 'arteries.'
- The French governor of Louisiana also founded the city of Detroit. General Motors named one of their best cars after him: the Cadillac. They named the Pontiac after the Ottowa Indian chief who led the siege of Detroit in the 1760s.
- When an Italian car company named their car the Fabrica Italiana Automobile Torino, it was shortened to the initials and called the Fiat.
- The Chase Manhattan Bank was named after Lincoln's Secretary of the Treasury, Salmon B. Chase.
- Broccoli comes from the Italian word *brocco* meaning 'little sprout.'
- Radish comes from the Latin *radix* meaning root.

Flower Facts

- 'Azalea' comes from the Latin word *azaleos* meaning dry or parched. The plant was so named in the belief that it grew only in dry soils.
- *Rhodon* is Greek for rose, and *dendron* means tree: rhododendron.
- Iris was the goddess of the rainbow. She was in charge of receiving the souls of dying women. The goddess Juno was so impressed with her purity that she named a flower after her.
- Lobelia was named in honor of botanist Matthias L'Obel.
- Marigolds were named after the Virgin Mary: Mary's gold.
- The wisteria vine was named after naturalist Dr. Casper Wistar.
- The Greeks thought that the leaves of the common garden flower alyssum could cure the madness caused by being bitten by a rabid animal. Since *lyssa* was the word for madness and "*a*" is a negative prefix, the alyssum was born.
- It was once believed that lupine destroyed the soil it grew in, so it was named after the wolf, *lupus* in Latin. Now we know that lupine just naturally grows best in soils that are already poor.

—Language—

- *Phlox* is the Greek word for fire, and phlox was named because of its fire red color. Phlox is also the root of the word phlegm, because phlegm was thought to cause the burning fires of fever and inflammation.

Mountain Flowers

- Columbine comes from the Latin word *columba* meaning dove because the flowers resemble a circle of doves.
- Larkspur was so named because the flower resembles the spur on the back of the feet of birds in the lark family.
- *Primus* is Latin for first, and primrose is one of the first flowers to appear in the spring.
- *Pasque* was a French word for Passover and Easter, and the Pasque flower was so named because it blooms around that time of year.
- *Penstemon* is Greek and means literally 'five stamens.'
- The ancient word *slyppe* meant dung. Cowslip is a plant that grows well in cow dung.

Plant Bits

- The Sanskrit word *parna* meaning a wing or feather became the German word *farn* which became the Anglo-Saxon word *fearn* and is now our fern.
- The Anglo-Saxon word *haeth* meant a wasteland, and gave us the words heath, heather, and heathen.
- Lichens come from the Greek verb *leichein* meaning 'to lick up,' because they seem to lick their way across the ground as they grow.
- *Mistel* is an old Anglo-Saxon word meaning dung, and *tan* meant twig. *Misteltan* or 'the little dung twig' was so named because birds eat the berries off the twigs and the seeds are deposited in their dung. Today the word has turned into mistletoe.
- *Wych* is Anglo-Saxon for 'to bend' and witch hazel is 'the bending hazel.'
- *Trunk* is the Latin word for tree, so 'tree trunk' is redundant. A traveling case

became known as a trunk because the first ones were made out of the hollowed out section of a trunk.

Herbs And Berries

- *Gar* is an old English word meaning spear, and *leac* is the original way of spelling leek. *Garleac* is now our garlic, a leek shaped like a spear.
- The Chinese word *jen-shen* meant 'man-plant,' referring to the shape of the root. It resulted in our word ginseng.
- Mentha was the mythical mistress of Pluto, ruler of Hades. Pluto's wife was so jealous that she transformed Mentha into a lowly plant that would forever afterwards be trampled upon by humans. Pluto felt sorry for Mentha, and decreed that the more the plant was trampled, the sweeter it would smell. Today, Mentha is called mint.
- Chamomile came from the Greek words *chamai* meaning 'on the ground,' and *melon,* meaning apple.
- The Spanish word *zarza* means a bramble, and *parilla* means a small vine. *Zarzaparilla* was translated into English as sarsaparilla.
- Strawberry comes from the old word *streaw* which means strew, because the plant reproduces by strewing its runners across the ground.
- Cranberries were originally called cranebarries because the stamens of the flowers look like the beak of a crane. Likewise, geraniums were named from the Greek word *geranos* meaning crane, because the seed pods are pointed like the bill of a crane.

Weed Words

- The German word *knobbe* means any knob or bump, such as the bud of the flower of what we now call knapweed.
- The Latin word *mollis* means soft, and gives us mullenweed, a tall plant with fuzzy soft leaves.
- Nettles were originally used to weave nets. The word net originates with the Sanskrit word *nahyati* meaning 'he binds.'
- Chickweed was given its name because chickens like to eats its leaves and seeds.
- The Latin word *purgare* means to purge, and spurge was named because the sap of the plant causes anyone who ingests it to vomit.
- The flowers of the toadflax have a mouth that opens like a toad's mouth when squeezed, and the stalks have leaves that resemble flax.

The Final Fact

The Latin words *de lira* mean 'out of the furrow.' Any farmer who let his oxen wander out of the furrow while plowing had to be 'delirious.'

FROGS

The First Fact

Handling a toad does *not* cause warts.

Toad Abuse

Cane toads are very large— sometimes as big as a frisbee— and they were imported into Australia from their native Central America to control the cane beetle, which was destroying the sugar cane crop. They failed to control the beetle because scientists forgot to note that the beetle is out during the day and the toad is only out at night. Cane toads nonetheless took a liking to the new continent and in short order had covered much of the area. The cane toad wards off predators by secreting a toxic goo from glands in its back. The poison contains the chemical bufotenine, which affects the nervous system. Scientists looking for a cure for mental disorders injected the compound into volunteer prisoners. The prisoners subsequently experienced hallucinations, nausea, and chest pains. The discovery focused attention on the cane toad as a hallucinatory agent, despite being outlawed by the Drug Enforcement Agency. Since then, many cases of toad abuse have popped up, prompting headlines such as, "How low will people stoop to get high?" and, "Toads take a licking from desperate druggies." Several people have died after licking toads. Reportedly, some dogs in Australia are addicted to toads. Research on toad venom continues, and a constructive use may yet be found for it one day.

Secret Weapon

If you were a frog who had just been caught by a snake who was intent on swallowing you, what would you do? Maybe you would release a bad tasting poison that would make the snake spit you out. Maybe you could tickle the snake's nose and make it sneeze. Or maybe you'd cause the snake to yawn, giving you the break you needed. This is the method used by the African clawed frog. The skin of this amphibian contains a compound that triggers uncontrollable fits of yawning and gaping in snakes. Furthermore, the snake's behavior resembles the involuntary muscle spasms of people who suffer from Parkinson's disease. Scientists are hopeful that this discovery may lead to a better understanding of the disease.

Sanitary Frogs

Researchers at the National Institute of Health were doing RNA studies on the African clawed frog. The experiments involved surgically removing the frog's ovaries, but what they accidentally discovered as a result of this surgery was more interesting than their original study. Researcher Michael Zasloff noticed that very few of the frogs developed infections resulting from the surgery, even though their aquarium water was surely contaminated with bacteria. Resulting investigations revealed that this species of frog has a natural antibiotic contained in the skin. The research team at the Health Institute has successfully duplicated the chemical and will soon begin tests on animals to determine if the effect of the compound will be as beneficial to other animals as it is to the frog.

Killer Frogs

Indians of South America are well known for hunting with poisoned arrows. The toxin is obtained from the skin of a number of brightly colored frogs commonly known as dart frogs. The most notable species is *Phyllobates terribiliss*. According to researchers, poison manufactured by this frog makes strychnine look like salt. When under stress, the frog secretes an oily poison from glands in its skin. By tormenting a single frog hunters can collect enough poison to dip about 50 arrows. The poison remains deadly for about six months.

Found only in Central and South America, these toxic amphibians are one of the most poisonous animals known to man. A single frog can produce enough poison to kill 20,000 mice, and it takes only .006 of an ounce to kill a 150-pound man. A single golden dart poison frog contains enough poison to kill 2,200 people. There is still no known antidote. Scientists are studying the substance, hoping it will help them discover clues to cystic fibrosis and other neurological diseases. Extracts may one day prove useful as heart stimulants or anesthetics. A hurdle standing in the way of research is the fact that dart frogs caught in the wild and held in captivity gradually loose their toxicity. Furthermore, dart frogs born in captivity do not secrete toxins at all. No one understands why this is.

Fast Facts About Frogs

- 'Amphibian' comes from the Greek words meaning 'two lives' since the frog can live both in water and on land.
- Frogs always croak, right? Wrong. The European tree frog sounds like a quacking duck. Another kind of frog sounds like a cat meowing.
- Frogs have no ribs.
- A frog closes its eyes by pulling the eyeballs deeper into the sockets. Its tongue is attached to the front of the mouth to give better reach. Do frogs have teeth? Just two tiny teeth in the upper jaw, which keep prey from getting away.

- A frog doesn't need to drink water because it absorbs water through the skin.
- A frog's thigh, shin, and foot are nearly equal in length, making jumping easier.
- A bullfrog with a six-inch body can leap ten times its own body length.
- Tadpoles are born one sex or the other, but environmental influences can change the frog's sex. If food is scarce or the temperature is not right, the transformation of female tadpoles into male frogs keeps the population down until conditions improve in the pond.
- Some frogs can live for 20 years. One toad lived 36 years.
- The world's largest frog was a Goliath frog of West Africa, measuring 32 inches and weighing just over seven pounds. On the other hand, the arrow poison frog of Cuba typically measures less than a half inch long.
- If you pick up a frog while you have insect repellent on your hands, the frog will absorb it through the skin and become very sick.

Famous Frogs

Mark Twain popularized frog-jumping contests in his story *The Celebrated Jumping Frog of Calaveras County*. Every year in May, residents of Angel City, California, stage a frog-jumping contest. How far can a frog jump? Actually, frog jumps are not measured on a per-jump basis, but by totaling the distance covered in three consecutive jumps. Rosie the Ribbiter, a "basic pond-variety frog," jumped 21 feet, 5 inches in 1986 to capture a national record. Another frog named Ex Lax made a single leap of 17 and a half feet for a single-jump world record. Scientists generally measure frog jumps in multiples of body length. One kind of cricket frog can leap up to 48 times its body length. Researchers recently discovered that because of poor vision, frogs aim for patches of blue when they jump, heading for sky or water. You can expect to see frog owners standing at the finish line wearing sky-blue clothing in the future.

From Eggs to Legs

Frogs always lay their eggs in ponds, right? Wrong!

- The Malaysian hill frog lives high in the mountains where there are few ponds, so it lays eggs in damp moss hanging from trees. The tadpoles live in the moss and develop into frogs there.
- One kind of dart frog lays eggs on moist vegetation, watching over the eggs until the tadpoles hatch. Then the young crawl up on the backs of either parent and are literally glued in place by a mucous secretion. They are attached there for more than a week, until the parent can find a proper pool to release them. The water loosens the mucous bond and the young swim free.
- A species of Costa Rican frog lives in the forest where ponds or streams are not easy to find. Female frogs lay eggs in moist moss or tiny spots of water that collect in plants. A remarkable adaptation allows these frogs to develop from egg to adult without passing through a phase as tadpoles. When the egg hatches, out comes a fully formed frog the size of a housefly.
- Bullfrogs can lay 20,000 eggs at a time. On the other hand, some kinds of dart-poison frogs will lay a single tiny egg in each of the miniature droplets that

forms when rainwater collects in the base of a leaf. The mother frog will also lay a number of unfertilized eggs next to the fertilized egg so the tadpole will have something to eat when it finally hatches.
- The leaf frogs in South and Central America lay their eggs between two leaves over a pond. The sticky stuff holding the eggs together also glues the two leaves together. The mother frog keeps the eggs moist by urinating on them. When they hatch, the tadpoles fall into the water.
- The male Darwin's frog scoops up all the fertilized eggs and holds them in his mouth. He holds them in his large vocal pouch while they hatch, grow, and turn into tiny frogs.
- The eggs of the marsupial frog are placed on the mother's back, where a pouch of skin grows around them to offer protection. Tadpoles hatch and develop in the pouch, completing their development into frogs without ever seeing water.
- The male midwife toad will wrap the long sticky strands of eggs around his legs, hopping around with them until they are ready to hatch. Only then will he deposit them in the water.
- The eggs of the leopard frog are white on one side and black on the other. The white part contains the genetic material; the black part contains a barrier to ultraviolet light. When exposed to light, the egg rotates the black side up, blocking the UV radiation and absorbing heat that helps with incubation.

Quick Bits

- Humans will die if they lose about 8% of their body water. However, the Western spadefoot toad of North America can lose 60% of its body water and still survive. This survival tactic gets the animal through dry spells. Many types of frogs can store extra water in their bodies to help get them through droughts, sometimes storing as much as half their weight in water.
- Frogs are green, right? Not always. Many frogs have nearly psychedelic coloring. There are pink frogs, blue frogs, yellow and purple frogs, and even a transparent frog. Glass frogs of South America have a skin that is so transparent that their heart, veins, and internal organs can be seen. The Malaysian flying frog changes color during the day, going from blue to green to black.
- Some tadpoles group up and swim in a tight clump around and around on the bottom of the pond. Scientists theorize they do this in order to stir up food from the bottom.
- What is the difference between a frog and a toad? A toad is a *type* of frog. Toads tend to live in the woods rather than near water. Their skin is thicker and bumpier than most frogs, and they tend to be fatter. When you find one frog, there are bound to be a lot of other frogs around, but toads generally live a more solitary life on land.
- One type of frog called the paradoxical frog is a foot long as a tadpole. It constantly shrinks as it grows older, ending up as a full-grown frog just over an inch long. The paradoxical frog lives on the island of Trinidad. Scientists in

the area, after observing a tadpole of such dimensions, were looking for a frog of truly monstrous proportions. All they could find was a tiny frog barely over an inch long. It was years before the connection was made.

Leaping Lizards? Flying Frogs!

Frogs always travel by hopping or swimming, right? Nope! In Borneo, one species of frog lives in the treetops but must breed in the water far below. Instead of bothering with a tedious hike to the bottom of the tree, these frogs simply spread their "wings" and fly on down. Webbed arms and legs allow the frog to fall in a controlled glide, spiralling down to the ground where there are important matters to attend to. In order to escape predators, the Malaysian flying frog can travel 50 feet in a single glide from one tree to another.

Borneo tree frog starts a lifetime tradition

How Did The Toad Cross The Road?

A problem in England concerns squashed toads. Toads come out at night and cross the road in search of mates. They always come out about the time of night that the pubs close, and many get squashed in spite of the warning signs along the highway. Now the Toads On Roads Committee comes out every night with flashlights and buckets to pick up the toads and deposit them safely on the other side of the road.

The Homing Instinct

Frogs, like salmon, always return to the place of their birth to reproduce. Even if the original pond no longer exists, frogs will die rather than travel to a different place to spawn. When a new road is built over filled-in ponds, the frogs die under the wheels of passing cars rather than move to another nearby pond. The Australian Transcontinental Railway has occassionaly been forced to stop because so many migrating frogs were getting squashed on the tracks that the wheels lost all traction.

Song Of Love

Gray tree frogs live in woodlands of eastern America. The female listens to the trilling call of males in the surrounding area. When she decides which male has the call she likes best, she hops up to him and nudges him with her nose, indicating her willingness to mate. But scientists were curious to find out what kind of a male frog's call was the most attractive to a female. The loudest? The longest? The nearest? Biologists set up a chamber with two speakers, putting one female at a time in the chamber. Each speaker emitted a slightly different mating call. They watched to see which speaker the females preferred. They discovered the pulse rate is the most important factor: females prefer males with a slow call. This may be because a different species of frog has a faster call. The next most important factor was the duration of the call. Females prefer longer calls over shorter calls. Longer calls require more energy expenditure, meaning that the female seems to want to push the male to his physical limit. Further research showed that some males win a mate without uttering a single call. They simply hang out next to a noisy male and grab the female as soon as she comes around.

Frog Futures

What is the frog's worst enemy? Snakes? Birds? Turtles? Nope— it's humans. Polluted water, bulldozed ponds, drained swamplands, blocked migration routes, and insecticide damage all contribute to falling populations and a potentially endangered animal. The destruction of the rain forests also spells doom for many species.

The Final Fact

Bangladesh exports so many frog legs that the population of the insects frogs usually feed on has skyrocketed.

KITCHEN

The First Fact
The average human eats about 70 tons of food in a lifetime.

Eating Your Words
In French, *hors* means outside and *oeuvres* means the works: literally 'apart from the main work.' Salad comes from the Latin *salsus* meaning salted. Cole slaw is a salad which comes from the Dutch term *koolsa*, meaning cabbage, and *sla* meaning salad. The French word for head, *caboche*, gave us our cabbage. *Spago* is the Italian word for 'little cord': spaghetti. The cantaloupe was first grown in Cantalupo, Italy, and brussels sprouts come from Brussels, Belgium. Gelatin, Jell-o, and jelly come from the Latin word *gelo*, meaning to congeal. *Desservir* is the French word for 'clear away,' and that's what you do before dessert is served. The land along the river Volga was known to the Greeks as the Rha. Since this was an unknown territory, they called it *barbaron*, or barbarian. A plant they found there was dubbed *rha barbaron*, meaning 'from the barbarian land of Rha.' Pass the word through Latin and into English, and you have rhubarb. If you're having tutti-frutti for dessert, you're using an Italian word for 'all fruits.' If you have some chocolate, you'll be using a Mexican-Indian word for bitter water, *chocolatl.* And if you're taking heat about the calories— well, calorie is the Latin word for heat.

Measure For Measure
When Fannie was in high school in the late 1800s she suffered a paralytic stroke which left her with a limp and forced her to stay home, where she cooked for boarders. Later she got a job as a nanny and acted on a child's suggestion to develop a system of measurements in cooking— tablespoon, teaspoon, etc. At the age of 30, Fannie enrolled in cooking school. She liked it so much she eventually became the head of the school. Soon she opened her own school, in which cooking was a standardized procedure with reliable measurements. Next she became a lecturer in great demand, and in 1896 she published a book on cooking. The popularity of this book was responsible for standardizing measurements in the kitchen. By 1977 *Fannie Farmer's Boston Cooking School Cook Book* had sold over four million copies.

The Man Behind Duncan Hines
In 1936 a man named Duncan Hines published a guide to the best restaurants along America's highways called *Adventures in Good Eating.* The American public was in a motoring craze, and the book sold millions of copies. Restaurants across the nation sported prominent signs saying "Recommended by Duncan Hines." In the 1940s a businessman named Roy Park came out with a new line of baked goods, and looked around for someone to endorse his product. Polls of housewives showed that the name Duncan Hines was more well known than that of the vice president of the U.S.— Alben Barkley— even in Barkley's home

state! In 1948 Duncan and Roy teamed up. Three weeks after the introduction of the new goods, they had swallowed 48% of the national market.

Tupperware

Earl S. Tupper was a chemist when he began working with a soft plastic called polyethylene in 1942. In 1945 he used it to produce an unbreakable bathroom tumbler. Next Tupper developed similar bowls, and also invented a new plastic cover with a seal that expelled internal air and created a vacuum. Tupper developed the idea of marketing his product through in-home parties rather than at the retail level. Within three years there were over 9,000 dealers giving Tupperware parties. Sales topped $25 million in 1954. When he sold out his interest in the company to Rexall Drugs in 1958, he received $9 million. He retired to Costa Rica and lived there until his death in 1983.

Tin Can Facts

One of Napoleon's biggest problems during his war campaigns was food. No matter how much his soldiers took with them, it spoiled. Villagers were unable to feed the large influx of people. Finally, Napoleon offered a big prize to anyone who could come up with a way to preserve food. Nicholas Appert had grown up working in his father's wine cellars, and had become a wine bottler and cook. He was intrigued with the idea that wine would never go bad if it was bottled correctly. He wondered what would happen to food if it were bottled as well. He tried soups and stews, then fruits, vegetables and milk. When the bottles were sterilized, filled, corked, and heated, the results were excellent. He took his discovery to Napoleon, and was awarded 12,000 francs. Appert had invented canning, although it was several more years before cans were used instead of bottles. It was several more years after *that* when the can opener was invented. Before then, it took a hammer and chisel to open a can. In fact, some people believe that the bayonet (invented in the French town of Bayonne) was developed not to spear people, but merely to open cans!

Tough Teflon

In 1938 DuPont chemist Dr. Roy Plunkett was experimenting with coolant gasses used in refrigerators and air conditioners. He removed a container of experimental gas from a freezer. Expecting to find a vial of very cold gas, he was surprised to see the gas had congealed, covering the interior of the flask with a solid waxy substance. Plunkett ran some tests and found the new material was impervious to chemicals and heat. He named it tetrafluoroethylene, shortened to teflon. Later he was inducted into the Inventor's Hall of Fame for inventing what is known as the slipperiest substance on earth— equivalent to two wet ice cubes rubbing against each other in a warm room. It has hundreds of uses but wasn't applied to pans until 1958. Teflon-coated pans were first offered for sale in the U.S. in 1960. During the middle of a blizzard in which 17 inches of snow fell, Macy's in New York City offered 200 stick-free teflon pans for $7 each. They sold out in two days. Today teflon is used in everything from space suits to computer chips to artificial hearts. Teflon coats 15,000 joints in the Statue of

Liberty to help prevent aging; it covers brake pads to reduce wear; and it coats light bulbs to minimize breakage. The only thing that destroys teflon is an SOS pad.

SOS Pads

In 1917 Edwin Cox was a door-to-door salesman in San Francisco. However, his aluminum cookware didn't sell very well. He needed a gimmick to get his foot in the door— a free introductory gift. Since he was selling pans, he decided to sell a method of cleaning them. In his kitchen he repeatedly hand-dipped small steel wool pads into a soapy solution and hung them out to dry. This free gift did the trick and opened doors, but the housewives liked the pads better than they liked the pans. So he gave up the cookware and went into the steel wool pad business instead. In need of a name, his wife suggested 'Save Our Saucepans' and the SOS pad was invented.

On A Roll

The first toilet paper on a roll was introduced in 1857. In 1907 at the toilet paper factory owned by Edward and Clarence Scott, a large uncut roll of defective toilet paper material was delivered from the mill. It was heavy and wrinkled and about to be returned when someone suggested marketing it as disposable 'paper towels.' Hotels, restaurants, and railroad stations bought them for use in restrooms, but homeowners generally continued to use cloth towels. Not until the price dropped to a quarter for 200 sheets in 1931 did ScotTowels become a regular household product.

The All-American Floor

In 1860 a British citizen named Frederick Walton made a resilient floor covering by oxidizing linseed oil with resin and cork dust on a flax backing. In

Latin, flax is *linum* and oil is *oleum,* so he named the product linoleum. Just about that time, Thomas Armstrong invested $300 in a machine that made cork stoppers for bottles. He hated to waste the mounds of cork shavings that were left over, so when he heard about the new floor covering that used cork, he revamped his business and was soon selling Armstrong Linoleum Flooring. He was the first person to introduce color and pattern to the American kitchen floor.

Why Aluminum Linoleum Never Caught On:

Dishwashers

Josephine Cochrane was the wife of a wealthy Illinois politician in the 1880s. She gave a lot of dinner parties, and got so fed up with her servants breaking her expensive china while washing it that she resolved to invent an automatic dish washing machine. The result of her woodshed tinkering was a crude but effective dishwasher. Her rich friends placed orders for their own machines. As word spread, hotels and restaurants (who dealt with volume dishwashing and expensive breakage) began to order them as well. At the 1893 Chicago World's Fair, she won the highest award. Eventually Josephine Cochrane's company merged with an Ohio manufacturer to become Kitchenmaid. Although they tried to market dishwashers to the average American housewife, hot water heaters at that time were uncommon. Home dishwashers did not become popular until the 1950s.

Dish Bits

- Fork comes from the Latin word for pitchfork, *furca.* Forks first appeared in the 11th century. Some clergy said forks were sinful because only God-given fingers were worthy of touching God's bounty.
- Spoons are much older than forks. Archaeologists have found spoons that are 20,000 years old. The word comes from the Anglo-Saxon *spon* meaning chip—a curved chip of wood dipped into a bowl. In the 1400s it was popular for Italians to exchange spoons with handles carved in the shape of an apostle. These apostle spoons became a standard baptismal gift, and a child born with a 'silver spoon in its mouth' meant that the family was rich enough to buy an expensive christening gift. It was also popular for lovers to exchange engraved spoons, hence our expression 'spooning.'

—Kitchen— 59

- The chief minister to France's King Louis III was disgusted by the practice of picking one's teeth at the table with a knife, so he ordered the servants to grind down the tips of all knives, thereby inventing the table knife. This eating implement caught on quickly as housewives strove to imitate the king. In 1669 the French government outlawed pointed knives altogether.
- The word bowl comes from the Anglo-Saxon *bolla* meaning round, and plate comes from the Old French *plat* meaning flat. The Sanskrit word *kupa* meant 'water well' and turned into the modern cup. The first crude British glass was green, and the Celtic word for green is *glas*. Table comes from the Latin *tabula* meaning board. This is where our phrase 'room and board' originates.

Quick Bits

- 46% of Frosted Flakes are consumed by adults.
- Spam controls 75% of the canned luncheon-meat market.
- There's been a 30% drop in consumption of white bread since 1977.
- Oreo cookies out-sell all other cookies worldwide.
- According to the U.S. Dept. of Agriculture, the following items are the ten most consumed foods in the U.S.: fresh milk, potatoes, beef, sugar, canned vegetables, fresh fruits, pork, chicken, eggs, and citrus fruits.
- 63% of women polled said they decide what to serve for dinner.
- The world's first TV dinner was Swanson's turkey, mashed potatoes, and peas. It appeared in 1953.
- 50% of Americans watch TV while eating dinner.
- Americans spend about $6 billion a year on snack foods, and only $5 billion on fresh fruits.

Fast Food Facts

- Baking dinner rolls used to be a lengthy process. Joe Gregor of Florida knew there must be a way of preparing rolls ahead of time so they could be popped into the oven just before dinner. In 1949 he experimented at length, to no avail. Then one day a few minutes after he put another experiment into the oven, the city fire alarm rang. Since Joe was a volunteer fireman, he had to respond. He yanked the rolls from the oven and went to put the fire out. When he returned, he found that the rolls were pasty and looked like plaster. Still, he baked them just to see how they turned out. Much to his surprise, they were delicious! Joe Gregor had finally discovered how to manufacture pre-made dinner rolls. Today we pop them into the oven ten minutes before dinner.
- Carl Smith was a General Mills executive when he took a train trip in 1930. He went into the dining car long after the dinner hour and was surprised when the chef served him a good meal along with piping hot rolls within just a few minutes. He went to ask the chef how he had been able to make fresh biscuits on such short notice. The chef explained that he always kept lard, flour, baking powder and salt blended in the ice box. Then all he had to do was pull out the mixture, add water, and pop it into the oven. Intrigued, Smith asked the research division of General Mills to come up with a way to package such a

mixture in a box. As a result, Bisquick was introduced to the public in 1931.
- In 1930 Ruth Wakefield worked at the Toll House Inn, located on a Massachusetts toll road. One day she decided to make chocolate cookies. After she had already mixed the dough, she discovered she was out of baker's chocolate to mix into the batter. Instead, she broke bits of semi-sweet chocolate into the dough, expecting the bits to melt into the batter and produce chocolate cookies. But when she pulled the cookies out of the oven, she found that she had accidentally invented chocolate chip cookies. Everybody liked them so much that the Toll House cookie industry was built around them. Today half the cookies baked in American homes are chocolate chip.
- Clarence was on a fur-trading expedition in 1912 when he decided to go ice fishing while it was 20° below zero. The fish he caught froze instantly when he removed them from the water. Back at camp, he tossed a fish into a bucket of warm water and was amazed to see it come to life again. After thinking about this, he concluded the fish survived because it had been frozen so quickly. This gave him an idea. He tried flash-freezing food with good success. In 1925 Clarence Birdseye marketed his first line of frozen food— fish.

The Final Fact

In a poll, most women said the maximum amount of time they wanted to spend making dinner was 30 minutes. Most men said 15 minutes.

GOLF

The First Fact

Astronaut Alan Shepard made golf history when he knocked a golf ball around on the moon. But he missed the first shot, taking a mulligan. This earned him a lifetime membership in the U.S. Duffers Association of Newport, Kentucky. They also awarded him the presidency of their first moon chapter.

Fantastic Shots

- In the course of the 1949 British Open, Harry Bradshaw accidentally drove a ball into a beer bottle. The ball broke the bottle's neck and ended up at the bottom of the bottle. Rather than risk a penalty, Bradshaw decided to play it where it lay. He whacked the bottle with his club. The ball traveled about 30 feet.
- In 1975 Perry Crowley of Connecticut was playing golf when he hit a ball into the water. It skipped off the lake, ricocheted off a rake in the nearby sand trap, landed on the green and skidded into the cup.
- During a 1938 PGA tournament, Jimmy Hine's chip shot on the 13th hole hit opponent Sam Snead's ball, and they both ended up in the cup. The players, who were tied, were each awarded a birdie two. Snead eventually beat Hines by one stroke.
- Songwriter Hoagy Carmichael was playing at Pebble Beach, California. He teed up on a par-three hole, chose a club, and smacked the ball. It bounced once on the green, rolled over to the pin, and dropped in the hole for a hole-in-one. Hoagy didn't react at all. He just reached into his pocket, pulled out another ball, teed up again, and said, "I think I've got the idea now."
- Henry "Dads" Miller of Anaheim, California, once shot a 99 on a 5,734-yard course. He was 100 years old at the time, and had not taken up golf until the age of 67.

Quips & Quotes

"If you watch the game, it's fun. If you play it, it's recreation. If you work at it, it's golf."
-*Bob Hope*

"Golf is an awkward set of bodily contortions designed to produce a grateful result."
-*Tommy Armour*

"Have you ever noticed what golf spells backwards?" -*Al Boliska*

"Golf is a good walk spoiled." -*Mark Twain*

"The only reason I ever played golf in the first place was so I could afford to hunt and fish." -*Sam Snead*

"I play in the low 80s. If it's any hotter than that, I won't play." -*Joe E. Lewis*

Wit Bits

- A golfer badly sliced his drive, and the ball crashed through the windshield of a passing car. The driver lost control and ended up in the ditch. When the cop arrived on the scene, he found the golfer standing next to his ball where it lay on the road. "What do you plan on doing about this?" asked the officer. "Well," replied the golfer, "for one thing, I plan on changing my grip!"
- "Why don't you play golf with Fred anymore?" a wife asked her husband one evening. "Would *you* play golf with a sneak who writes down the wrong score, and moves his ball when you aren't looking?" "No," said his wife. "Well," said the husband, "Neither will Fred."
- A woman was questioning why her husband was getting home so late from golfing. He replied, "On the 13th hole, Don had a heart attack, and from then on it was, hit the ball and drag Don...Hit the ball and drag Don..."

Fast Facts

- A regulation golf ball can weigh no more than 1.62 ounces and cannot be larger than 1.62 inches in diameter.
- Most golf balls have 332 dimples. They are usually .013 inches deep. The dimples help give backspin.
- A golf club remains in contact with the ball for only a thousandth of a second and travels with the ball for three quarters of an inch.
- A good tee shot produces backspin around 60 revolutions per second. This means that a 220-yard drive will travel more than three feet before it has completed one revolution.
- After a good shot, a golf ball can reach speeds up to 250 m.p.h.
- The world's record drive traveled 430 yards. A more typical well-hit tee shot can still travel a distance equal to the length of the *Queen Elizabeth,* one of the world's largest oceanliners, at 345 yards.
- The bulk of a golf ball is made up of a rubber thread stretched to 285 yards, or approximately the length of a typical tee shot. When hit well, the energy stored in the thread is enough to raise a 150-pound man off the ground to a height of two feet. The force exerted on the inner core equals about 7,500 pounds, or the weight of an average car.
- The center of most golf balls is filled either with water or a mixture of castor

—Golf—

- oil and silicone.
- A player can have no more than 14 clubs in his golf bag.
- The golf equipment industry in America accounts for about $600 million in sales each year.
- An 18-hole golf course can require up to a million gallons of water a day.
- The world's longest golf hole is the seventh hole (par seven) of 909 yards at the Sano Course, Satsuki Golf Club, Japan.
- 400 million rounds of golf are played in America each year.
- *Golf Digest* reported that there were 43,386 hole-in-one shots made in 1985. That averages out to 119 per day.

Fact

A woman who played in the 1912 Shawnee Golf Invitational for Ladies sent her ball into the Binniekill River at the 16th hole. Her husband rowed a boat a mile downstream until she finally was able to smack the ball out of the water, where it landed in a thicket. By the time she worked herself back to the cup, she had racked up 166 strokes.

Golf Through History

- Golf was originally a game played by the Romans called *pagancia*. It involved hitting a feather-filled leather ball with a crooked stick.
- Golf was popular with the Scots. By the mid-1400s it had become so pervasive that King James II outlawed the game because he felt his subjects were wasting too much time playing it when they should be doing useful things. Archers were losing their shooting ability because they were spending so much time hitting little balls around instead of practicing their aim.
- Golf was once an Olympic sport. It was dropped in 1904.
- The first golf tee was patented on December 12, 1889 by G. F. Grant of Boston.

The Golfer's Wife

- Golfer: "My wife says if I don't give up golf, she'll leave me." Caddy: "That's terrible!" Golfer: "I'll say! I sure will miss her!"
- Wife: "Golf, golf, golf! That's all you ever do! I'd drop dead if you ever spent a day at home!" Hubby: "Now, now, honey— you know I can't be bribed!"
- A golfer of sorts in Calcutta / Thought of curses too pungent to utter / When his wife, as he found / Ere commencing a round / Was beating a rug with his putter.
- Two men were golfing when a funeral procession came by. One man removed his hat and held it over his heart. The other man said, "I didn't know you were so patriotic— that was very respectful." "Well," replied the other man, "she was a good wife. We were married for 25 years!"

A Great Invention

The year was 1927. Garnet Carter was a real estate man who owned a hotel on the top of Lookout Mountain in Tennessee. He was looking for an added attraction to entertain his customers. He came up with a successful idea that immediately caught on: miniature golf. It could be installed in a week and cost (at that time) as little as $2,000. The first one ever built on Long Island brought in $362 on its first day of business. At first they were barred from within 50 feet of churches, schools, or hospitals. But one progressive church in New Jersey installed its own course and urged everyone to come. The profits paid off the church's debts. Three years later, there were 40,000 miniature golf courses across the country and Garnet Carter was a rich man. The  industry took in $225 million in a single year, and employed 200,000 people. The Queen of Belgium got hooked, and even Al Capone invested in it. The steel industry, the pipe industry, and the felt industry were very happy— and so was Garnet Carter.

Quick Bits

- Stephen Horchler of Scotland invented a golf ball that has a built-in radio transmitter that beeps distress signals so golfers can track it.
- According to *Sports Illustrated*, the Ralph Marlen Fish Tie Company markets six different neckties depicting common golf scenes. One tie shows the putter about to make a five-foot putt; one shows a ball teetering on the lip of the cup; and another depicts the 19th hole— a few drops of Tabasco being added to a Bloody Mary. All of the ties are made of 100% polyester.
- Crows living near the golf course in Bombay, India, have developed a taste for golf balls. They pick up the balls and take them back to their nests. Caddies run after the balls and cover them with a red cloth before the crows can get there.
- Sign posted on an African golf course: "If the ball comes to rest in dangerous proximity to a crocodile or a hippopotamus, another ball may be dropped."
- On a golf course in Africa, golfers tee off from the flat top of a 15-foot termite mound. Other mounds on the course provide the hazards.
- You need to walk 35 miles to reduce one pound of fat. If you drink two average cocktails during an 18-hole round of golf, you will end up with a net caloric gain.
- In the movie *Diamonds are Forever*, James Bond smuggled diamonds inside his golf balls.

Famous Golfers

- Dwight Eisenhower enjoyed golf and was criticized for spending too much time on the course. Bumper stickers appeared saying, "Ben Hogan for President. If We're Going to Have a Golfer, Let's Have a Good One." One critical senator suggested that a fund be set up to protect squirrels from Ike's flying golf balls. Once Ike appeared wearing a wrist brace and explained to a visitor that it was due to a mild arthritic condition. The visitor remarked that he was glad it wasn't serious. Ike replied, "I should say it *is* serious! It means that I can't play golf!" After he left office, someone asked him if it had affected his golf game. "Sure has," he replied. "A lot more people beat me now!"
- When Laura Baugh started tearing up the golf courses in the early 1970s, she was still too young to play on the women's pro tour according to regulations. So her agent took her to Japan, which did not have a minimum age requirement. The golf-happy Japanese fixated on the curvaceous young blond American. Laura Baugh photos, calendars, photo albums, cosmetics, school supplies, English-language cassettes, sports clothing, and gold accessories were all the rage in Japan. She became the highest paid female golfer even though she had never played in an American tournament.
- Fred Astaire was nearly as good at golfing as he was at dancing. In his 1938 film *Carefree,* he danced over tables, down the hallway, out to the terrace, and onto a golf course. There he was to dance over to a golf club and hit— in rhythm and on cue— a dozen golfballs that were lined up on the fairway. When the crew went to retrieve the golf balls, they found all twelve balls within eight feet of each other on the green.
- Someone asked Muhammed Ali how he fared at golf. "I am the greatest," he replied. "I just haven't played yet!"
- Australian actor and playwright Oscar Asche was playing a pretty bad game. Finally he hit a good shot and said to his caddie, "I guess you've seen worse players than me." The caddie did not reply. Assuming he hadn't heard, Asche repeated the remark. "I heard you before," replied the caddie. "I was just considering."
- Golfer Tommy Bolt, after missing six putts in a row, shook his fist at the sky and yelled, "Why don't You come down here and fight like a man!" Another time during a golf clinic he asked his 14-year-old son to "show the nice folks what I taught you." His son obediently hurled his nine iron into the sky.
- President Gerald Ford was playing golf with hockey star Gordie Howe. Howe conceded a two-foot putt to Ford at the 12th hole, but Ford insisted on taking the shot. He missed. "We won't count that one," said Howe. "Maybe *you* won't count that one," said Ford, turning to survey the crowd of reporters and Secret Service men, "but *they* will!"
- Golfer Gene Sarazen was playing in an early world championship match in 1922 against Walter Hagen. At the end of the first day, he was two strokes behind, on account of missing a couple of easy putts due to nerves. That night

he complained of stomach pains and was unable to sleep. Nevertheless, the next day he went on to win the match. Four hours later he underwent an emergency appendectomy. He commented, "A sick appendix is not as difficult to deal with as a five-foot putt."
- Golfer Sam Snead was granted an audience with Pope John in 1961. He confessed to the monsignor that he had brought along his putter, hoping the Pope might bless it. The monsignor nodded in sympathy, commiserating, "My putting is absolutely hopeless, too." Snead concluded, "If you *live* here and can't putt, what chance is there for me?"

Caddie Jokes

- *Caddie:* someone who stands behind a golfer and didn't see the ball either.
- Beginner: "How do you like my game?" Caddie: "It's all right, but I still prefer golf."
- A golfer teed up, looked over to the next green, and told the caddie, "That's good for one long drive and a putt." He swung hard, managing to move the ball only a few feet off the tee. The caddie handed him his putter and said, "Now for a heck of a putt."
- The beginner teed up for the fifth time, gave a violent swing, and watched as a small object whirled away. "I finally got that ball off!" he cried jubilantly. "Mister," replied the caddie, "That was your watch."

The Final Fact

In 1987 Vice President Dan Quayle played an average of three golf games each week.

JEWELS

The First Fact

Herb Bales, a jeweler in Fairfield, Ohio, had two diamonds set in his top front teeth.

The Value Of Diamonds

A diamond resists acids, can penetrate steel, and has the best thermal conductivity of any material known. Diamonds etch, grind, groove, polish, and sharpen. They drill for oil, cut cataracts from eyes, and chop spaghetti into uniform lengths. They cut everything from marble to fish, and groove runways and roads to prevent skidding. Every car coming off the line in Detroit has consumed a carat and a half of diamonds that have been used to polish pistons or round window glass. Contact lenses are ground with diamonds, and a single piece of diamond sandpaper can polish 10,000 Tupperware bowls.

In 1978 NASA needed a small window for a space probe to Venus. The window had to withstand four months of the vacuum of space, travel through incredible extremes of heat and cold, hold up under tremendous deceleration forces, keep out the highly corrosive gasses of Venus, and withstand atmospheric pressures 100 times greater than Earth's. Only diamond would do.

Stories Of Jewels And Gems

- During the Depression, Harpo Marx disguised himself and went to Tiffany's to look at jewels. He acted very suspiciously, then furtively started heading for the door. The police were immediately summoned, whereupon Harpo broke into a run, tripping and falling. When he fell, dozens of "jewels" fell out of his pockets, scattering over the street. Panic ensued until it was revealed that the "gems" were simply cut glass. It had all been a practical joke.
- Locomotive salesman Diamond Jim Brady owned quite a collection of diamonds in the 1880s when they were still a curiosity. He was a show-off where his jewels were concerned, which was a fact that got him many hard-to-come-by appointments with railroad magnates interested in seeing his diamond collection. He showered gems on his girlfriend Lillian Russell, giving her a diamond-encrusted bicycle and a diamond-studded chamber pot with a large eye at the bottom.
- In 1872 two hucksters from Kentucky decided to cash in on the diamond fever recently caused by a big diamond discovery in South Africa. They were California prospectors who had seen what the cry "Gold!" could do— so they decided to cry "Diamond!" After pooling their money of $75,000, they went to London and purchased a quantity of poor quality, uncut diamonds, emeralds, sapphires, and rubies. They scattered them on the ground in a desolate area near the Colorado-Utah border, and then convinced a group of wealthy San Fran-

cisco bankers that they had found a fabulously rich diamond field. The men offered to guide the bankers to the location, but in order to keep the location secret, they insisted the bankers be blindfolded. The bankers fell for the hoax hook, line, and sinker. Soon newspapers all over the country heralded the find, and a corporation was set up with investors sinking $80,000 each into the venture. Mining engineers were called to the scene; jewelers tested the gems and found them authentic; Congressmen became involved; and the whole thing could have been very embarrassing if the head of the U.S. Geological Survey hadn't mentioned that it was geologically impossible for diamonds, rubies, emeralds, and sapphires to be found together in the same rock formation. When a geologist went to the site with some investors, they found a partially cut and polished diamond laying on the ground along with the rough diamonds. The hoax was exposed, but not before the perpetrators escaped with some $600,000.

Inept Hoaxsters

Fast Facts

- 80% of diamond yield is too poor to classify as gem quality.
- Most diamonds are between 80 and 800 million years old.
- The U.S. consumes 50% of the world's diamond production.
- Diamonds that are dark blue, dark red, or dark pink are worth in excess of a million dollars per carat. A quality clear diamond retails for around $30,000 per carat.
- The Hope diamond is the only natural deep blue diamond ever found.
- A .87 carat red diamond which sold at auction for $1,200,000 was originally sold in Billings, Montana for $3,000.
- Rubies and sapphires are the second hardest natural substances on earth.
- Australia has surpassed South Africa as the leading diamond producer.
- The only diamond mine in America is in Arkansas.
- Diamonds are simply crystalized carbon (like coal or soot) and will burn at a temperature of 1652°F.
- The first instance of a diamond being given as a symbol of marital commitment was when emperor Maximilian I gave a diamond ring to his fiancé Mary of Burgundy in 1477. She died before the wedding.
- 97% of people picking an engagement ring choose a diamond.
- When Richard Burton bought Elizabeth Taylor a 69.40 carat diamond for $1 million, thousands of people waited in a line that stretched for blocks to see it in the window at Cartier's.

Historical Gems

- The Kohinoor diamond is one of the world's largest and has a history dating back centuries. The name means "mountain of light" and it was felt that whomever owned the gem ruled the world. It's been traced back to the 1300s, but it's history gets interesting in 1739 when it was owned by Mohammed Shah of India. Nadir Shah, leader of the Persians, invaded the country and seized the national gems from Mohammed Shah. But the Kohinoor was not there. For months he ransacked Delhi, killing thousands of men, women, and children in his effort to find the prized gem. When terror failed to produce the stone, he got crafty and questioned favored members of Mohammed's harem. One of the women revealed that Mohammed kept the diamond wrapped up in his turban at all times. Rather than simply kill him and seize the Kohinoor, the Nadir instead declared peace, vowed eternal friendship to Mohammed, and threw a big celebration with Mohammed as guest of honor. As a binding gesture, he insisted on exchanging turbans to seal the friendship. Mohammed Shah gave up his turban without batting an eye, losing the diamond but keeping his life. Nadir Shah got his in the end, though— just a few years later, he was assassinated. Centuries later, the Kohinoor fell into British hands when Punjab was annexed to the British Empire. It was presented to Queen Victoria and is now displayed with the Royal Crown Jewels.

- In 1701 a slave found a huge diamond while working in a mine in India. Risking his life to smuggle it out, he slashed his leg open and hid the stone in the wound. After fleeing to the coast, he made a deal with a ship captain for safe passage to another port in exchange for half of what the diamond would bring. Once out to sea, the slave "fell" overboard and drowned. The captain sold the gem for $5,000 and it fell into the hands of an Indian merchant, who offered it to Thomas Pitt, governor of Madras, for a half million dollars. Pitt, guessing the diamond was stolen, drove a hard bargain and acquired it for only $100,000. After cutting and polishing, Pitt sold it to the Regent of France and made a profit of over a half million dollars on the deal. His fortune was made— a fortune that was passed on to his heirs, including William Pitt, after whom Pittsburgh, Pennsylvania was named.

- Cecil Rhodes was a sickly English boy, so his parents sent him to the healthier climate of South Africa where his brother had a cotton farm. Discouraged by poor crops, the brothers turned to diamond mining instead, hoping to make a fortune. It took years, but Cecil finally succeeded. He formed the DeBeers Mining Company, which still controls much of the diamond market. In 1891 Rhodes controlled 90% of the market. Rhodesia was named for him. Fabulously wealthy when he died, he left his fortune in trust to be used for scholarships for bright young people— Rhodes scholars.

- In 1905 in South Africa, a mine superintendent was preparing to close the mine for the day when he saw a glint. It turned out to be the largest diamond ever found. Named the Cullinan after the mine's founder, it weighed in at 3,106 carats. (The average engagement ring diamond is around half a carat.) Before

faceting, it was the size of a man's fist and weighed over a pound. It was cleaved into nine separate gems.
- Aga Khan, leader of the Ismaili Moslems, turned 75 years old in 1946. To celebrate his birthday, wealthy Moslems in Bombay volunteered to contribute to his favorite charities an amount of money equal to his weight in diamonds. Aga Khan sat on a giant balance scale while case after case of diamonds were loaded on the other side. The diamonds were of industrial quality to lower their value, but it still took over a half million carats at a value of $1.5 million to counterbalance Aga Khan's hefty 243 pounds.

Ignominious Defeat

In 1981 Francois Mitterand was elected president of France. His win might be attributed in part to actions of his opponent, incumbent President Valery Giscard d'Estaing. Three times in the 1970s Giscard accepted gifts of diamonds from the Emperor of the Central African Empire. When a newspaper found out, Giscard claimed the diamonds had all been donated to museums. The newspaper checked but could find no such museums. Giscard then went on television and said the diamonds had been sold and the money was given to the African Red Cross. The paper checked but found no gifts to the Red Cross. Giscard then said they had been sent to the Emperor's successor in Africa. The paper found that Giscard had actually sent the equivalent of one small diamond to Africa. After his defeat in 1981, a crowd surrounded him shouting, "Give back the diamonds!"

Sapphires In Montana

Yogo Gulch in central Montana yields fine and famous gems. Like most famous discoveries, it was accidental. In the late 1800s Jake Hoover was caught in a rainstorm while prospecting. He took refuge from the rain under a rock ledge. While waiting for the weather to clear, he picked up some gravel, which he later panned in nearby Yogo Creek. It contained a little gold, so he filed a claim. While working the site, Jake found some pretty pebbles. He sent some gold with a few of the stones to a former girlfriend in Maine. He was surprised a few weeks later to receive a letter from her thanking him for the sapphires. His reaction reportedly was, "What the heck is a sapphire?" After a Helena jeweler assured him of their value, he sent a cigar box full of the pebbles to Tiffany's in New York, who responded with a check for $3,750 and a request for more. Yogo sapphires were born.

Quick Bits

- Charlemagne forbad the custom of burying jewels with the dead, feeling that precious stones should be worn and enjoyed by the living.
- In 1534 Pope Clement VII lay dying. Physicians of the day felt that jewels crushed to a fine powder had curative powers. In the few days before he died, physicians poured doses worth 40,000 silver coins down his throat, all to no avail.
- The largest sapphire ever found was 2,302 carats, discovered in Australia in 1935. It was carved into a bust of Abe Lincoln.
- The largest recorded crystal of gem quality was a 520,000 carat aquamarine found in Brazil in 1910.
- A 14 pound pearl was found in a giant clam off the Philippines.
- The largest single quartz crystal weighed in at over 1,000 pounds.
- Turquoise is a very porous mineral and is sensitive to chemicals. It should not be brought into contact with soap or detergent. Its color may fade if exposed to light.
- Carat comes from *carob*, a small Oriental bean. The beans are remarkably uniform in size and became a standard for weighing gems.
- Crystal comes from the Greek word *krystallos*, meaning ice, because the ancient Greeks thought that transparent rock crystals were frozen water turned to stone.
- The word diamond comes from the Greek word *adamas* meaning 'unconquerable.'

Antics & Anecdotes

- One family went on a vacation to Singapore and the husband treated the wife to a beautiful diamond ring. Just before they landed, she took off the ring and hid it in her bra. While passing through customs they said they had nothing to claim. At that point, their young son piped up, "Oh, Mama, you forgot about the ring in your bra!" Customs officials took them aside and called in the appraiser. After a while he said with a smile, "You owe us nothing. You've been sold a fake!"
- Elizabeth Taylor's diamond ring was noticed by Princess Margaret, who remarked that it was a bit vulgar. Taylor handed the ring to the Princess to try on. "There, it's not so vulgar now, is it?" said Taylor.
- Lady Heathbottom wore a famous strand of pearls to a fancy party, when a woman she knew said maliciously, "What lovely pearls! Are they genuine?" She nodded. "Well," said the uppity woman, "You can always tell by biting

them. Here, let me try." "Certainly," replied Lady Heathbottom, offering the pearls, "but remember, you can't tell real pearls with false teeth!"

- Louisine Havermeyer was a noted art collector. She was approached by a wealthy woman, bedecked with jewels and pearls, who scornfully inquired why Mrs. Havermeyer spent so much money on dabs of paint. Mrs. Havermeyer examined the lady's pearl necklace for some time before replying, "I prefer to have something made by a man than to have something made by an oyster."

Quick Bits

- Diamonds, sapphires, and garnets are all found in a rainbow of colors.
- Rubies and sapphires are identical except for color. They are made up of aluminum and oxygen: aluminum oxide.
- Quartz is the most common mineral on earth. Chemically, it is the oxide of the element silicon. There are many forms of quartz. Amethyst is quartz colored purple through a combination of iron and irradiation. The name comes from the Greek word for 'not drunk' because it was thought that amethyst would nullify the effects of alcohol. Tiger eyes, agates, and jasper are forms of quartz. The opal is a close cousin.

Quips & Quotes

"The demand for diamonds is based on vanity."   *-Harry Oppenheimer*

"Many speak the truth when they say that they despise riches, but they mean the riches possessed by other men."   *-Charles Caleb Colton*

"Banks and riches are chains of gold, but still chains."   *-Edmund Ruffin*

"It is better to have old secondhand diamonds than none at all." *-Mark Twain*

The Final Fact

One night in 1983 Eric DeWilde of Florida was searching for his missing bike. Next to the railroad he found a bag of diamonds and jewelry which had been partly crushed by train wheels. Because no owner could be found, the gems were auctioned at Christies. The boy received all proceeds totalling some $350,000.

HOLLYWOOD

The First Fact

Hollywood was named in 1883 when Mr. and Mrs. Wilcox moved from Kansas to some California farmland which they purchased for $1.25 an acre. Mrs. Wilcox named the place Hollywood after her two pots of English holly she had brought with her.

Frankenstein Facts

- The make-up for Frankenstein's monster is copyrighted by Universal Studios and can't be duplicated without their permission.
- Director Mel Brooks bought up the old sets and lab equipment that were used in the 1931 film *Frankenstein*. He used the stuff in the spoof *Young Frankenstein*.
- Boris Karloff starred as the original Frankenstein's monster but he received no screen credit. When the credits rolled, only a large question mark appeared beside the monster's name. Bela Lugosi had been offered the part but refused because it wasn't a speaking role.

Oz Bits

- Shirley Temple was originally scheduled to star as Dorothy in *The Wizard of Oz* but she was under contract to 20th Century Fox, and they asked MGM for too much money. Judy Garland was hired instead. She was paid $300 per week for her work.
- Liza Minnelli, daughter of Judy Garland, married Jack Haley, Jr, the son of Jack Haley— who played the Tin Man.
- Margaret Hamilton, who played the wicked witch, was once a kindergarten teacher. During the filming of her witch appearances in *Oz*, she was badly burned by some special effects flames that melted her green copper make-up. It took her three months to recover.

Jaws Facts

- Steven Spielberg was only 26 when he directed *Jaws*.
- Peter Benchley, author of the book *Jaws*, appeared in the film as a reporter.
- Shark experts were hired to film a 25-foot great white shark for the movie, but they couldn't find any sharks that big. They could only find some 15-foot sharks. So they hired an ex-jocky named Carl Rizzo who stood only four feet, nine inches tall. He was given a specially made diving suit and small shark cage. The 15-foot sharks looked much bigger when they appeared next to this diminutive man.

Misc. Bits

- When Maurice Barrymore died, the straps around the coffin became twisted as the coffin was lowered into the grave. It had to be raised again to straighten things out. As the coffin reappeared, Lionel Barrymore nudged his brother John and whispered, "How like Father— a curtain call!"
- Producer Joseph Mankiewicz was making a movie of F. Scott Fitzgerald's

Three Comrades when he called up the author. He insisted the film would make more money if the female heroine did not die at the end of the movie, and he asked Fitzgerald to change the script. Fitzgerald retorted, "How about Romeo and Juliet— you wouldn't have wanted Juliet to live, would you?" "That's just it," replied the producer, recalling the dismal failure of the 1936 film version of the play. "*Romeo and Juliet* didn't make a cent!"

- Goldwyn and Mayer, producers who teamed up with Metro to form MGM, did not like each other much. Once after a noisy altercation, a friend chided Goldwyn about the fight. Goldwyn protested that he and Mayer loved each other dearly. "We're like friends, we're like brothers. We love each other. We'd do anything for each other. We'd even cut each other's throats for each other!"
- Nunnally Johnson was a screenwriter. When someone asked him how he would adjust his writing to adapt to a wide screen, he replied, "Very simple. I'll just put the paper in sideways."
- Fred Astaire and Ginger Rogers danced the number "Cheek to Cheek" in the movie *Top Hat* while Rogers wore a dress covered with feathers. The dress had been made hastily, and as Astaire whirled her around the dance floor, feathers came flying off until the air looked like a pillow fight was in progress. The feather dress went back to the seamstresses, who used more glue and more feathers. During the second take, fewer feathers flew off, yet it was still quite noticeable. By the third take, enough glue had been used so that only a few feathers came loose and cameramen were able to film around them.

Chaplin Facts

- Charlie Chaplin once entered a Charlie Chaplin look-alike contest in Monte Carlo. He came in third.
- Charlie Chaplin made 35 films in the year 1914 alone.
- Playwright Charles MacArthur was once picking Charlie Chaplin's brain about how to write humor. "Is a fat lady slipping on a banana peel still funny?" he asked. "If so, should I show the lady, then the banana peel, then the fall; or should I show the banana peel, then the lady, then the fall?" "Neither," replied Chaplin. "First you show the fat lady approaching; then you show the banana peel; then you show the fat lady and the banana peel together; then she steps *over* the banana peel and disappears down a manhole."

Laurel And Hardy Facts

- Stan Laurel and Charlie Chaplin shared a room in a boarding house when they first arrived in the U.S. Cooking was not allowed in the room, so Chaplin would play the violin or cello to cover the sound of Stan frying food on a secret hot plate.
- Oliver Hardy originally played villains in movies before teaming up with Stan Laurel.
- Stan Laurel's real name is Stan Jefferson. He changed it because it had 13 letters in it, an unlucky number.

Fast Facts About Actors

- Lucille Ball was once dismissed from a drama class because the instructor said she was too shy.
- Clark Gable flunked his first screen test because directors thought his ears were too big.
- Lou Costello (of Abbott & Costello) was once a prizefighter. Bob Hope was also once a boxer. Rock Hudson was once a mailman.
- Robert Redford's nose has been broken five times.
- There were two hippopotami present at the second wedding of Elizabeth Taylor and Richard Burton.
- Horror actor Bela Lugosi was buried in his Dracula cloak.
- Boris Karloff turned down the part as the "Invisible Man" because he didn't want to be unseen until the end of the movie.
- Marlene Dietrich played the musical saw.
- Warren Beatty and Shirley MacLaine are brother and sister.
- Fred Astaire insured his legs for a million dollars. Betty Grable insured her legs for one and a quarter million. Jimmy Durante insured his nose for $100,000.
- *Captain Blood* starred Errol Flynn. The sequel, *Son of Captain Blood* starred his son, Sean Flynn.
- Mel Blanc, the voice for cartoon character Bugs Bunny, was allergic to carrots.

Before appearing in The Exorcist, *Linda Blair appeared in a mustard commercial on TV.*

Epic Movies

- In the 1959 movie *Ben Hur*, a chariot comes racing around a ring, only to find a wrecked chariot blocking the path. The driver jumps over the wreck with his chariot, falls out of the chariot, then pulls himself back in. This stunt happened entirely by accident, but the cameras got it on film and it was so spectacular that it was included in the final cut.
- In *The French Connection*, an area of Brooklyn was roped off before filming the car chase, but a truck slipped through the barricades and hit a speeding car.

It was captured on film. The driver was paid for the damage to his truck and the scene was left in the movie.
- In the original *Ten Commandments* the scene where the Red Sea closes over the pursuing army and washes the horses away in a flood was done with double exposures. The first shot was of the horses running, panicking, and rearing. The second shot showed Jell-O with water running over it. The effect was so realistic that the Society for the Prevention of Cruelty to Animals thought that real horses had been drowned. The director had to show them the double exposure.
- After filming *King Kong,* Fay Wray had to go into the sound studio and record an extra five minutes of screaming so the sound technicians could splice it into the film where needed.
- The battle scene in *War and Peace* used 12,000 men and 800 horses.
- The makers of *Gone With the Wind* originally planned to use several thousand dummies for the scene that shows acres and acres of wounded Confederate soldiers. However, the Screen Actor's Guild protested so loudly that they were forced to hire 3,000 extras to lay on the ground for the scene. They still needed a couple thousand dummies to fill in the far shots. The movie lasts 222 minutes, and all but 30 minutes have music in the background. During the scene where Atlanta burns, old sets from the movies *Last of the Mohicans, King Kong, The Garden of Allah* and *Little Lord Fauntleroy* were all set on fire.

Tarzan Facts

- The Tarzan yell is based on a yodel Johnny Weissmuller learned from his father as a child. The yodel is played backwards and speeded up to three times its normal rate.
- Johnny Weissmuller was an Olympic swimming champion modeling swim suits when a talent scout found him and offered him the part of Tarzan. It is said

that when he was asked to do a screen test for the part of Tarzan, Weissmuller replied, "Me? Tarzan?"

Hitchcock Bits

- Alfred Hitchcock's habit was to put in a brief appearance in each of his films. It was a hard stunt to pull off in the movie *Lifeboat* in which only a very few characters appear. But sharp-eyed observers noticed that when a lifeboat occupant picked up a newspaper from the bottom of the boat, Hitchcock appeared on the back page of the paper in a weight-loss advertisement. He was in the "before" and "after" pictures in the ad.
- In the film *The Birds,* live birds were strapped to the backs of children. When the kids ran out of the schoolhouse with birds on their backs, the birds tried to fly away, found themselves trapped, and began to peck at the children. This is exactly what director Alfred Hitchcock was striving for.

Fields Facts

- W. C. Fields was once hired to be a professional drowner. The owner of a concession stand in Atlantic City, New Jersey hired Fields to swim out in the ocean, pretend to be drowning, be rescued by a lifeguard, and then be revived. A crowd would gather to watch the drama, and the concession owner sold them all hot dogs, ice cream, and drinks. He split the profits with Fields.
- Fields once spiked Baby Leroy's bottle with booze because the kid co-star was stealing too many scenes. The rest of the day's shooting had to be called off when little Leroy started staggering around drunk.

Fast Facts

- When the script called for Claudette Colbert to take a bath in 400 gallons of milk in the 1932 film *The Sign of the Cross*, she agreed to do the scene. Unfortunately, the scene took a week to complete and by the end of the week, the 400 gallons of milk had gone sour.
- There are lots of theaters across the country named the Roxy. That's because a man named Roxy built what was then the world's largest theater in New York City. The place had a hospital, six box offices, a radio studio, an apartment for Mr. Roxy, an orchestra of 110 musicians, five organists, and a corps of ushers said to be ex-Marines.
- Nothing can be used in place of beer in films. Nothing looks like beer except beer.
- During the filming of *Casablanca*, no one knew how it was going to turn out. The writers were writing it as fast as it was filmed.
- The film *Madame Butterfly* was banned in Japan because part of the heroine's naked elbow shows up in the film, considered obscene then.
- Cowboy star Tom Mix drove around in a white limo that had a large pair of steer horns attached as a hood ornament. Mix suffered 26 different injuries in the course of his film career. Before becoming an actor, Mix served as a sheriff, a deputy U.S. Marshal, and a Texas Ranger.
- During the filming of *Bonnie Prince Charlie*, David Niven was in a sword fight

with an actor when he accidentally tripped, plunging his sword deep into the thigh of his screen opponent. He quickly pulled the blade out, and the man limped away. Niven insisted the man see a doctor. Only then did the guy roll up his trouser leg, revealing that he had an artificial leg. He lost the real leg in a battle.

- Harold Lloyd did all his own stunts. In 1920 a prop bomb went off unexpectedly, blowing off Lloyd's thumb and forefinger. From then on he wore a rubber glove to hide the handicap.
- Paul Newman was so embarrassed by his acting in his first film *The Silver Chalice* that he ran a newspaper ad asking folks not to watch it.
- Jean Harlow died in the middle of filming the picture *Saratoga*. The studio finished it by using a double named Mary Dees.
- While on the set of *The Goldwyn Follies* in 1937, ventriloquist Edgar Bergen and his dummy Charlie McCarthy were to do a scene. But no matter how many times they tried it, the sound just didn't come out right. Whenever Bergen spoke, the sound was fine. But when the dummy replied, the sound faded out. No one could figure out the problem. Finally someone on the set realized that the sound man would point the mike at Bergen when Bergen spoke, but would then turn the mike towards the dummy to catch the dummy's reply.

Award Facts

- In 1934 MGM got mad at their star Clark Gable because he was asking for too much money. As punishment they loaned him to Columbia Pictures. The result was *It Happened One Night* which won an Oscar, made a clean sweep of Academy Awards, and was voted Best Picture.
- Will Rogers was the host of the 1933 Academy Awards. He called Best Actress nominees May Robson and Diana Wynyard to the stage, and everyone assumed it was because they had tied for the award. But Rogers gave them each a kiss, then announced the winner was Katharine Hepburn for her part in *Morning Glory*.
- During World War II the Oscar statue was made out of plaster because metal was an essential wartime material.
- When Walt Disney went to collect his Academy Award for the film *Snow White and the Seven Dwarves* he was handed one regular sized award statue and seven little tiny ones.
- When 10-year-old Tatum O'Neal appeared to accept her Academy Award for her part in *Paper Moon,* she wore a tux. She was the youngest person ever to win an Academy Award.

The Final Fact

There are over 20,000 famous animals and pets of movie stars buried in the L.A. pet cemetery.

TRIVIA

The First Fact
A wheeled office chair will travel an average of eight miles yearly.

Sports Facts

- A company in Portland is manufacturing hiking shoes using recycled sawdust, metal shavings, disposable diapers, coffee filters, foam rubber, and other bits of garbage. The product is called Deja Shoe.
- Two-piece suits are now legal in professional women's swim competitions.
- If ping-pong players in a professional tournament are using white balls, the players are not allowed to wear white shirts.
- Polo players are not allowed to play left-handed because it's too dangerous.
- The only sport more popular with women than men is gymnastics.
- In 1871 there were only 84 professional baseball players in the U.S.
- When Reverend James Curtin of England, received a special Christmas bonus from his congregation, he used it to bet on a football game. He won $100,000.
- Football is listed as the most dangerous game by *The Encyclopedia of Sports Sciences and Medicine.* The AMA reports that 46% of all college football players are injured during a typical season.
- Forest Peters of Montana State University drop-kicked 17 field goals in a single game in 1924.
- Before modern rules were adopted in wrestling, a lock hold could be maintained for hours. Wrestling matches sometimes lasted up to 11 hours.
- Wrestler William J. Cobb of Macon, Georgia, weighed in at 802 pounds, the heaviest wrestler on record.
- In tennis, 'love' means 'no score.' It comes from the French *l'oeuf* meaning egg, slang for zip, zero, zilch.
- When roosters fight, the loser flattens down the crest of feathers on his head. Thus the phrase 'crestfallen.'
- Basketball player John Mayson of Lincoln University once tipped the basketball into the wrong basket. His team lost 66-60 to Delaware State.
- Vern Mikkelsen of the Minneapolis Lakers fouled out of 127 NBA games, setting a record.
- In ancient times, fighters used to spit on their hands before the fight because saliva was thought to have magical powers.
- Don Sydner is the world champion spitter, having achieved a distance of 25 feet, 10 inches. He received a gold-plated spittoon as a prize.
- Chuck Linster of Wilmette, Illinois, was 16 years old when he performed 6,006 consecutive pushups.
- Lee Travino was teed up at the 13th hole in a tournament at Houston's Champions golf course when he was surprised to see a ball drop into the cup. It had been hit by pro golfer Bob Rosburg who had just teed off the 12th hole—and hit a hole in one on the wrong hole.

Made in the Shade

When a friend of Harvey Schakowsky developed skin cancer, Schakowsky was alarmed. He learned that one way to prevent skin cancer is by wearing protective clothing. "What *is* protective clothing?" he asked his friend. Nobody knew—not even doctors and specialists. So Schakowsky decided to look into the matter. Testing different fibers, he found that a typical cotton t-shirt will block only 50% of harmful rays from the sun. After some experimenting, he developed a fabric that blocks 99% of ultraviolet B radiation and 93% of ultraviolet A rays. It's made of a synthetically woven nylon treated with a patented chemical substance. Schakowsky is marketing the line as Solarweave, selling hats, jackets, and shirts. Schakowsky would eventually like to see all Little League and other sports players wearing his weave. He's also pushing for all clothing to be labeled telling consumers what protection, if any, they offer.

Animal Facts

- Yarrow's spiny lizard lives in the mountains of Arizona. The lizard has a third primitive eye on the top of its head. Researchers theorized that this 'parietal' eye was a sort of navigation system for the lizard. To test the theory, they captured 40 lizards and painted over the third eye. They released these 40 'blind' lizards along with 40 normal lizards 90 miles from where they'd been caught. The unpainted lizards began to head home in half an hour, but the painted lizards wandered around in circles. This confirmed that the third eye is key to a lizard's sense of direction.
- How do you vaccinate a fish? It's pretty difficult to catch them one at a time and give them shots, and introducing the medicine to their tank water doesn't allow them to absorb enough to be effective. But researchers at the University of Maryland and at MIT found that hormones and medications released in a tank of water will be absorbed up to 20 times better if ultrasound waves are sent through the water for about 15 minutes. Ultrasound apparently alters the permeability of fish skin and gills, allowing substances to be absorbed more easily.
- Researchers interested in the memory of honey bees did some experimenting. First they extracted proteins and molecules from the brains of bees that had learned to find their way back to their hives. Then they injected the stuff into the brains of bee embryos. The amazing result showed that after hatching, the baby bees were able to find their way back to the hive after being transplanted a mile away—even though they had not previously explored the area. Baby bees that had not received the transplanted hormones could not find their way home.
- Turkey vultures migrate each year, and many migrate to Florida to spend the winter. When the Dade County Courthouse was constructed near a favorite roosting spot, the vultures decided to roost on top of the new high-rise building. They like it there because they can spread their wings and step off the roof into a thermal updraft, gliding effortlessly away. They eat at a nearby garbage

dump. Often there are as many as 300 vultures on the roof of the skyscraper, prompting many jokes concerning the kinship that exists between the vultures and the lawyers occupying the building.
- Lately some people have been fitting their horses with tinted contact lenses. The lenses impair the ability of the horse to see well by cutting out some light. As a result, the horse picks its head up higher, opens its eyes wider, and keeps its ears forward— a perky, alert look that judges at horse shows are attracted to.
- Grieved over the death of your pet? Now you can send your pet's ashes, along with photos of the deceased animal, to a company in Grand Rapids, Michigan. There the ashes are mixed with clay, poured into a mold of the animal, and made into a life-like sculpture of the pet. Prices start at around $500.

Quick Bits about Medicine

- 98% of Americans suffer from some tooth decay.
- Penicillin is fatal to guinea pigs.
- Rhesus monkeys fed a typical American diet died within two years.
- 75% of the food Americans eat is processed before being consumed.
- An eight inch stalk of celery contains about five calories. It takes more calories to chew, swallow, and digest it than that.

There are some 700 Americans living now who were conceived in a test tube.

Medical Facts

- Patients dying of terminal illnesses at St. Patrick's Hospital in Missoula, Montana, have their passage into the next life eased by harpists, singers, and other musicians who are on call to provide peaceful background music. The Chalice of Repose Project was formulated by Therese Schroeder-Sheker, a former music professor who was appalled to see how callously dying patients were treated. She explains that the music reduces pain, slows vital signs, and decreases agitation.
- According to an article in *Omni* magazine, cinnamon boosts the effect of insulin

activity by nearly 1,200%. Even a half teaspoon of cinnamon taken each day can dramatically lower the need for insulin by making it more effective. Researchers hope that one day this information will be used to allow diabetics to take less insulin, which will result in fewer medical emergencies due to elevated insulin levels.
- The best hangover preventative seems to be a large glass of orange juice taken with a pain-killer such as aspirin before going to bed. Sixty test subjects who each drank two bottles of champagne felt better the next morning after drinking juice than a control group who did not.
- A shrub found in West Africa yields a hallucinogen called ibogaine that natives use to get in touch with dead ancestors. Howard Lotsof was a heroin addict in 1962 when he tried out ibogaine, looking for a new high. After coming down off his 36-hour psychedelic trip, he found that he no longer craved heroin. He was surprised that he experienced no withdrawal either. He gave ibogaine to six other heroin addicts, and five of them also lost their desire for heroin. Lotsof patented the use of ibogaine for treatment of drug addictions, and began looking for researchers to investigate its potential. One researcher found that lab rats with free access to morphine reduced their intake after just one injection of ibogaine. Further research showed that ibogaine curbs the rise of dopamine in the body. Dopamine is a neurotransmitter that plays a key role in addiction. Many drugs trigger the release of dopamine, and dopamine causes a euphoric feeling. But ibogaine somehow blocks the release of dopamine for several days or weeks. Having kicked his addiction, Lotsof is now pushing for human testing of ibogaine. He admits that one major problem could be that most drug addicts don't really want to stop.

Fast Facts About Drugs

- Worldwide, 5% of the population abuses drugs. Of those people, 50% are found in the U.S.
- About 20% of Americans drink alcohol once a week or more. 5% are heavy drinkers.
- In 1981 police arrested less than half a million people for drug violations. In 1991 they arrested over a million.
- In 1980, 27% of people serving time in federal prisons were there because of drug offenses. In 1989, 49% were.
- Annually there are over 400,000 emergency room admissions due to drugs.

Misc. Bits

- More than three times as many boys as girls are dyslexic.
- More boys are nearsighted than girls.
- Two-thirds of first-time astronauts flying in the space shuttle experience motion sickness and nausea.
- The life span of a taste bud is ten days.
- About 40% of the native population of Papua New Guinea enjoy a genetic mutation that makes them resistant or immune to malaria.

—Trivia—

Quick Bits About Animals

- A dog has 17 muscles in each ear.
- A typical 100-ton blue whale will eat about four tons of krill daily.
- The single thread making up the cocoon of a silk worm is about a mile long.
- The common midge, a tiny bug, can beat its wings 133,000 times per minute. This is the fastest physical action in the entire animal kingdom.

More people walk to work in Alaska than in any other state.

Nature Bits

- Raindrops can fall at a maximum of 22 m.p.h.
- The oceans contain enough salt to cover all of the continents with salt to a depth of 500 feet.
- Sick plants run fevers— their temperatures run a degree or two higher than healthy plants.
- If the world's total land mass were equally divided among the world's population, each person would have 8.5 acres.
- The earth spins 1,000 m.p.h. faster at the equator than at the poles.

Altered States

- Dale Kaczmarek takes people on tours of Chicago. What makes his tours more interesting than others is that he takes his tourists only to places reputed to be haunted, such as Resurrection Cemetery, the Indian Burial Grounds, and various houses and businesses in the area. He reports that there are over 150 locations in the Chicago area that are said to be haunted, giving him enough material for years of tours.
- Yoga is a system of stretching and relaxation techniques. In the town of Toccoa, Georgia, commissioners voted seven to one to outlaw yoga lessons sponsored by the city's recreational department. The reason was because local fundamentalist Christians thought yoga was a heathen activity similar to devil worship. Said one local objector, "Yoga has hidden behind a veil of innocence... They get you to meditate and leave your mind blank. When that happens, you... open yourself up to demonic invasion and spirits." The mayor objected and called for a public hearing, where townfolk came out resoundingly in favor of yoga. Classes continued a week later. Publicity surrounding the episode caused attendance to double. Mayor Harris reports, "No sign of the Devil. I keep looking, but I don't see any horns."

Presidential Facts

- George Clinton served as vice-president under two different presidents: Thomas Jefferson and James Madison.

- Four different presidents served as representative, senator, and vice-president before becoming president: John Tyler, Andrew Johnson, Lyndon Johnson, and Richard Nixon.
- Only one First Lady has been born outside the U.S.: Louisa Johnson was born in London and married John Quincy Adams in 1797.
- Alexander Hamilton's casket cost $25 and was paid for by the State of New York.
- Grover Cleveland got fewer popular votes when he won the election in 1884 than when he lost the election in 1888.

Misc. Bits

- The U.S. accepts more immigrants annually than the other 179 nations of the world combined.
- One-third more oil spills occur on Saturdays than any other day of the week, due to increased boat traffic, reduced staff, and 'weekend psychology.'
- Robots in Japan pay union dues.
- Central Park in New York City is almost twice as big as Monaco, which is the second smallest country in the world.
- It takes 11.5 days for a million seconds to go by, but 32 years for a billion seconds to pass.
- If there are ten books on a bookshelf, they can be arranged in 3,628,800 different ways.
- Today an astronaut can reach the moon in less time than it took a stagecoach to travel the length of Great Britain.

The Final Fact

Mouse sex lasts five seconds.

ICE CREAM

The First Fact

The American ice cream industry produces enough ice cream annually to fill the Grand Canyon. Each American eats an average of 23 quarts of frozen dairy products yearly. We consume more ice cream per capita than any other nation.

Ice Cream Through History

- Hippocrates wrote, "It is dangerous to heat, cool, or make a commotion all of a sudden in the body... Why should anyone run the hazard in the heat of the summer of drinking iced waters which are excessively cold, and suddenly throwing the body into a different state than it was before, producing thereby many ill effects? But, for all this, people will not take warning and most men would rather run the hazard of their lives or health than be deprived of the pleasure of drinking out of ice."
- Fifty years before Christ, Nero sent teams of runners into the mountains for snow, which was brought to his table flavored with honey and fruit juices.

- When Catherine de'Medici married the future King Henry II of France in 1533, she celebrated with a forerunner of ice cream: fruit ices. The wedding celebration lasted a month, and each day her chefs served a different flavor.
- The story goes that in Britain in the 1600s, King Charles I was so happy when he first tasted "cream ice" that he gave the chef who made it 20 pounds sterling each year on the condition that the recipe be kept secret. After Charles was beheaded in 1649, the chef sold the secret to a collection of rich men.
- The first ad for ice cream appeared in the *New York Gazette* in 1777.
- A record of George Washington's expenses included the purchase of "a cream machine for ice" bought on May 17, 1784.
- In 1846 Nancy Johnson invented the first hand-cranked ice cream freezer. She never patented it. In 1848 William Young registered it with the Patent Office. He had the decency to name it the Johnson Patent Ice-Cream Freezer.

- Ice cream cones were rolled by hand until Frederick Bruckman of Portland, Oregon invented the cone-rolling machine in 1912. A decade later, one-third of all ice cream consumed was eaten on top of cones.
- In 1935 Pres. Franklin Roosevelt admitted that he ate ice cream every day.
- The sales of ice cream skyrocketed from five million gallons a year in 1899 to 30 million in 1909, and 150 million in 1919.

World Records

- Tony Dowdeswell ate three pounds, six ounces of ice cream in 31.37 seconds on July 16, 1986, in Dowdeswell, Gloucestershire, England.
- The largest ice cream sundae weighed about 55,000 pounds. It was made by Palm Dairies of Edmonton, Alberta in July of 1988. It contained about 45,000 pounds of ice cream and another 10,000 pounds of syrup and miscellaneous toppings.

Fountain Of Youth

In 1934 the movie *Kid Millions* starring Eddie Cantor was released. Twenty million moviegoers were treated to a color talking picture featuring an ice cream fantasy as a finalé. The scene occurred in an ice cream factory where chorus girls carried chocolate and strawberries to a huge freezer while other scantily clad girls skated across the freezer and coasted around on large slabs of Neapolitan. Meanwhile Cantor was treating hundreds of ragged children to an ice cream banquet, and a reformed gangster shot cherries into each kid's dish from a machine gun.

Just Desserts

In 1851 a milk dealer named Jacob Fussell sat down to figure out what he could do with all his surplus cream. Ice cream was his solution, and he soon found that he was making more money dealing in frozen dairy products than in milk. By 1856 he had become the nation's first ice cream wholesaler. Soon his factories were popping up across the country. Fussell found himself with what nearly amounted to an ice cream monopoly, and he tried to fix the price of a quart at an outrageous $1.25. Retailers revolted en masse. Fussell was quickly brought back down to earth, and the price of ice cream dropped.

Cold War

- During the Korean War, General Lewis Puller announced that it was ridiculous to pamper marines with ice cream. He demanded that the Armed Forces serve troops beer and whiskey instead. The Women's Christian Temperance Union howled, enlisted men howled, and the Pentagon announced that ice cream would be served in Korean mess lines three times a week.
- During World War II, destroyers were rewarded with 20 gallons of ice cream for every pilot they pulled out of the water.
- When the aircraft carrier *Lexington* was damaged and the order was given to abandon ship, someone mentioned that the ship was carrying a lot of ice cream. Sailors ate as much as they could before going over the side of the ship.

- A Navy PX operator stationed in New Hebrides got a hold of an ice cream freezer. He used local fruits and flavors to invent exotic ice creams. His name was Burt Baskin, and he went on to co-found Baskin-Robbins.
- British airmen put ice cream mixtures in cans in the rear compartments, where the plane's vibration combined with freezing temperatures at high altitudes would yield delicious ice cream.
- In 1941 the Tokyo warlords pronounced ice cream a needless luxury and dropped the price so low that it forced vendors out of business. The following year shortages of milk and sugar were so acute in Britain that ice cream was banned outright.
- In 1946 consumption of ice cream in the U.S. was twice the pre-war level.

The Ice Age

- The cone is thought to have originated at the St. Louis World's Fair in 1904. Ernest Hamwi was a concessionaire selling a waferlike pastry baked on a waffle iron. Next to his stand was an ice cream vendor selling scoops in small disposable dishes. When he ran out of containers, Hamwi came to the rescue by rolling his wafers into a cornucopia horn and putting a scoop of ice cream in its mouth.

- The generally accepted story of the birth of the ice cream soda concerns Robert Green, who was dispensing soda drinks at a Philadelphia festival in 1874. The drink he was selling was a mix of cream, syrup, and carbonated water. When he ran out of cream, he substituted ice cream instead. Green had averaged $6 a day with his original drink, but was bringing in $600 a day selling the world's first ice cream sodas.
- Christian Nelson was working in a candy store in 1919 when a boy ordered an ice cream sandwich, but changed his mind and ordered a candy bar. Nelson wondered why you couldn't offer both treats in one. After experimenting with ice cream and melted chocolate, the Eskimo Pie was born. Nelson patented the idea, convinced it would make him rich. Unfortunately, he was not much at marketing and the business floundered. He was racking up balls in a pool hall for cash when he met up with a man named Stover. Stover was superintendent at an ice cream factory and together he and Nelson put the bar on the market. At one point they sold a quarter of a million bars in a single day in Des Moines. By 1922 a million pies were being sold daily across the country, and Nelson was raking in $30,000 a week in royalties. Then franchises stopped paying royalties and vendors impinged on the patent. By 1923 the company was going broke spending $4,000 a week to defend the patent. Russell Stover sold his share of

the company to Nelson for $30,000, using his money to open the first Russell Stover Candy Store. Meanwhile Nelson teamed up with R. S. Reynolds of the U.S. Foil Company. The distinctive foil wrapper was born. The combination became wildly successful.

- In 1890 sucking soda on the Sabbath was considered by some preachers to be sinful. They felt that sinners would spend the Sabbath in soda parlors instead of church. Soda at that time was considered to be nearly as evil as liquor. Evanston, Illinois had the distinction of being the first community to pass a law against the "Sunday Soda Menace," making it illegal to consume soda on Sunday. To bypass these blue laws, the sundae was invented. When you take an ice cream soda and remove the soda, you have ice cream and chocoate syrup left. Since it contained no soda at all, it was not against the law. It was originally spelled Sunday, but was changed to sundae to avoid being sacrilegious. Evanston, Illinois and Norfolk, Virginia both claim they were the first to invent sundaes.

- After trying out an Eskimo Pie, lollipop manufacturer Harry Burt wondered if he could improve on the design. Handing an early attempt to his daughter to sample, she pronounced it good, but too messy. She suggested he put it on a stick like his lollipops. The ice cream bar was born, and Burt named it the Good Humor. He applied for a patent, and three years later it had not come through. So Burt sent his son to Washington with a bunch of ice cream bars. After passing them out free to patent office officials, the patent was granted. Soon Good Humor trucks were standard in all major cities. The company got a big boost in Chicago in 1929. Seems the mobsters demanded $5,000 for protection—or else. The company refused the ultimatum, and doubled the insurance on the trucks. The next week eight Good Humor trucks were blown up. The insurance paid off and Good Humor was on the front page all over the country, boosting sales. The Good Humor company marked one out of every 12 sticks a "Lucky Stick" entitling the finder to a free ice cream bar. In 1938 the Federal Trade Commission ruled this an illegal lottery and outlawed it.

Fact

After Eskimo Pies were invented, demand for chocolate-coated novelties lifted the cocoa-dependent economy of Ecuador out of the gutter.

Fast Facts

- Dr. David Reuben, author of *Everything You Always Wanted to Know About Sex* etc., maintains that the way to a man's heart may be through his stomach, especially if you serve him lots of milk products, including ice cream. Reuben

states, "When a woman establishes herself as a provider of milk, she literally makes herself part of her man's unconscious mind. If she wants him to marry her, all she has to do is inject enough milk into their relationship."
- In 1952 at Yale, the police ordered a portable ice cream cart off the campus. The resulting riot involved 1,500 students and was quelled with hoses and clubs. The owner of the pushcart was ultimately allowed to return to campus and a victory rally was held in his honor.
- One ice cream novelty that never made it was ice cream in an aerosol can. Then there was the cone with a side-pocket for an extra scoop built in. The ice cream telegram made an appearance— a molded ice cream replica of a Western Union telegram, delivered to the home.
- Several years ago Ben & Jerry's ice cream company was forced to clean up their act. The ice cream slop that had previously been dumped into the sewers of Waterbury, Vermont was no longer allowed in the municipal sewer system. Managers brought in 300 pigs and fed the slop to them. The program was a success. However, the pigs refuse to eat chocolate mint chip ice cream slop.

A La Mode

Vanilla, chocolate, and strawberry are the three favorite flavors, in order. Vanilla accounts for 51% of ice cream sold, chocolate 13.5%, and strawberry 6%. Among sherbets, orange captures 40% of the market. In 1967 Fidel Castro boasted that his country would soon be able to make more flavors of ice cream than the U.S.'s paltry offering of 31. Irv Robbins of Baskin-Robbins immediately informed Castro's Minister of Information that Baskin-Robbins had nearly 300 flavors but customarily kept only 31 in each store.

Quick Bits

- In 1951 the ice cream industry lobbied to get a commemorative postage stamp celebrating the 100th birthday of ice cream. The effort failed.
- New Englanders eat almost twice as much ice cream as Southerners do.
- Ice cream contains 12% fat.
- An ice cream bar is 20% sugar, but Sugar Smacks cereal is 61% sugar.

Quips & Quotes

"There is something about hard times that brings out an urge for simple pleasures like ice cream." *-Wm. Holmes, manager, Beatrice Foods*

"In these harsh and uncertain times, as the establishment cracks and institutions crumble, it is no wonder we reach out to ice cream. It is a link to innocence and security, healing, soothing, wholesome..." *-Gael Greene*

"[Ice cream is] a relief from reality, a throwback to the childhood and a less complex world." *-Metro Boston*

"We dare not trust our wit for making our house pleasant to our friends, so we buy ice cream." *-Ralph Waldo Emerson*

"Ice cream, to my mind, is a symbol of American living."
-Thomas D'Alesandro, Jr.

Wit Bits

- There's a cannibal with a sweet tooth—for dinner he always has a Good Humor man.
- Hear about the man who crashed into the playground fence? He thought he was following a white line, but actually it was a Good Humor truck leaking vanilla.

Peach Mitchell

Dame Nellie Melba was a famous opera singer around the turn of the century. Her real name was Helen Porter Mitchell, but she adopted the name Melba because she was from Melbourne, Australia. In an interview, she was asked how she kept her figure slim. She replied that she enjoyed eating very dry toast with simple spreads. And so melba toast was born as housewives all over the world strove to imitate the star. At the same time, Auguste E. Scoffier, a famous French chef, had just received the Legion of Honor for his culinary achievements. He admired Melba's voice so much that he created a combination of peach and ice cream and served it to her after a performance of *Lohengrin*, naming it Peach Melba in her honor.

The Final Fact

The trademark of a dairy in Memphis was a four-leaf clover. In 1924 they advertised a free pint of ice cream to anyone who sent in a four-leaf clover. 50,000 arrived on the first day. The offer was quickly canceled.

NAMES

The First Fact

'Mister' comes from the Latin word *minister*, meaning a servant. But the original abbreviation 'Mr.' stood for the Latin word *magister* meaning chief or head. Mistress, from which we get Mrs., was originally the feminine form of magister.

Fast Facts

- No one on the *Mayflower* had a middle name. It wasn't the style back then. Of our first 17 presidents, only three had middle names. Of the next 18, only three did *not* have middle names.
- Shakespeare popularized the names Jessica, Bianca, Beatrice, Olivia, Rosalind, and Sylvia by using them in his plays.
- In the year 1185 the most popular boy's names were (in order): William, Robert, Richard, Ralph, Hugo, Walter, Roger, John, Geoffrey, Gilbert, Thomas, Henry, Adam, and Simon.
- In Britain in 1583 the most popular girl's names were: Jane, Elizabeth, Margaret, Ann, and Mary. In 1783 the most popular names were Mary, Ann, Elizabeth, Sarah, and Margaret. In 1965 they were Jane, Mary, Elizabeth, Sarah, and Ann.
- The Oregon state registrar reported that in 1986, 183 boys were christened Adam, but not a single girl was named Eve.
- The parents of Lyndon Baines Johnson couldn't agree on a name for their boy, so for the first three months of his life, LBJ was nameless.
- When Mr. and Mrs. William Claus of Marshall, Missouri, had a baby boy in 1888, they christened him Santa. Not only was he regularly deluged with letters from children, but he had trouble cashing checks, getting through to people on the phone, and registering at hotels.
- Mr. & Mrs. Piano of San Francisco named their child Grand.
- French music teacher Alphonse Durand named his kids Doh, Ray, Me, Fah, Soh, Lah, Te, and Octave.
- Mr. and Mrs. Henry Drabik of Chicago christened their daughters Marybeth, Marykay, Marysue, Marylynn, Maryjan, Marypat, and Maryrose. When their eighth child turned out to be a boy, they called him John Henry.
- Mr. & Mrs. Jack Trees of Firwood Place in Forest Park, Ohio, named their kids Merry Christmas, Jack Pine, and Douglas Fir Trees.

Twin Bits

- 62% of twins have names that start with the same initial as the other twin; 17% have names with a strong similarity; and 21% have names that are not related at all.
- The *New York Times* reported in 1965 that a set of triplets born in New Guinea were named Namba Wan, Namba Tu, and Namba Tri.

- Suggested names for triplets are Kate, Duplicate, and Complicate.
- When twins were born around midnight to a couple in England, the oldest was named Tuesday and the youngest Wednesday.
- When a clergyman was ready to baptize a pair of twins, he asked the nervous father what names they were to have. "Steak and Kidney," he replied. The mother interjected, "He means Kate and Sidney."
- Dick Gregory, a comedian who fought for equal rights for blacks in the South, named his twins Inte and Gration in 1964.

Surnames In America

- *Sur* comes from the Latin word *super* and means 'above and beyond.'
- The 2,200 most popular surnames in America are used by half of the people. To name the other half, there are over a million names.
- In 1974 the Social Security Administration had 1,286,556 different names on its rolls. It was not a complete list because the computer printout listed only the first six letters of each name, so Hernan would be listed the same as Hernandex, Hernando, or Hernani. Also on their roster were 448,663 one-of-a-kind names.
- More American last names start with the letter S than any other letter. B comes in second, M is third, and K is fourth. X starts the least names, preceded by U, Q, J, I, and Y.
- The Amish forbid marrying outside the sect, so there is no infusion of outside names. Most of the Amish share only seven different names. 50% of Amish people are named either Stolzfus, King, or Beiler. Just 20 names account for 96.7% of names used by Amish in Pennsylvania. One postman had 437 people named Stolzfus on his route.
- Cohen is the most common Jewish surname in the U.S. In New York City, there are more Cohens than there are Smiths.

John Smith

- The ten most common surnames in the U.S. are Smith, Johnson, Brown, Williams, Jones, Miller, Davis, Martin, Anderson, and Wilson.
- The Social Security Administration has 2,382,509 Smiths on the rolls.
- Smith County, Kansas is the geographic center of the U.S., and Smith Center is the county seat. If all the Smiths joined hands to form a circle with its center in Smith County, the circle would reach central Nebraska on the north, the Oklahoma line on the south, Denver on the west, and Topeka on the east.
- John is the most popular boy's name of all time. Johnson, meaning son of John, and Jones, being a contraction of Johnson, are two of the most popular surnames.
- In Russian, the name Ivan means John. The most common surname there is Ivanov, meaning Johnson. Petrov (Peterson) comes in second.
- A jury impaneled in St. Louis in August of 1965 had 12 men on it who were all named John. The alternate was also named John.

Famous Names

- Paul Revere's father's name was Rivoire, but he changed it to Revere so people could pronounce it.
- Winston Churchill, the statesman, was often confused with Winston Churchill, the writer. The writer was the better known at first because his novel *Richard Carvel* was very popular at the turn of the century. Winston Churchill, the statesman, began signing his name Winston S. Churchill to avoid confusion.
- When Chinese newspapers in Formosa needed to translate John Kennedy's name, they used three characters pronounced Kan Nai Dai, which mean "willing-endurance-bliss" in their language.
- In 1933 when Hitler became chancellor of Germany, there were 22 different people named Hitler listed in the New York City telephone directory. Twelve years later, there were none.
- Adolf Hitler's half brother, Alois Hitler, changed his name to Hans Iller in 1948 to get away from the Hitler stigma.
- There is no such person as Ellery Queen. The mysteries are actually written by two people, Frederic Dannay and Manfred B. Lee.

Foreign Facts

- In Holland, the cuckoo clock in a voting place was stopped on election day because it sounded like the name of the party leader, H. Koekoek.
- The ten most common Spanish/Mexican names found in the U.S. are Garcia, Martinez, Gonzalez, Lopez, Hernandez, Rodriguez, Sanches, Perez, Ramirez, and Flores.
- There are only about 200 different surnames commonly used in China today. It's estimated that 40% of the Chinese population have a last name of either Chang, Chao, Chen, Chu, Ho, Hsu, Hu, Li, Liu, Wang, or Wu.
- In some places in India, boys must be given names that have an even number of syllables, and girls must have an odd number of syllables.
- Confucious is the Latin form of the Chinese name K'ungfutse, meaning 'Master K'ung.' It was a fancy name given to the honorable K'ung Ch'iu.

Origins Of Last Names

Snyder is Dutch for taylor. Hoffman is German for farmworker. Webb, Webber, and Webster are German for weaver. Wagner was one who built wagons. Schultz is German for foreman or overseer. Vaughn is Welsh for little. Lloyd means gray; Reid means red; Schwartz means black; Calvin means bald; Mussolini means gnat; and Poe means peacock. Shafer, in all its different spellings, is German for shepherd. The Sheaffer Pen Company noticed that 9% of people writing to the company spelled the name wrong.

Notes On Names

Beethoven is Dutch for beet field. Brahms means son of Abraham. Tschaikovsky means one who came from the town of Czajkow. Chopin is French for fighting man. Dvorak means an attendant at a court. Schubert and Schumann both mean shoemaker. Verdi means green.

True Names

Goforth & Ketchum were a police team in Long Beach, California. *Heywood Tipsy* was arrested for drunk driving in Los Angeles. *M. Balmer* was an embalmer in Fort Collins, Colorado. *W.A. Coldflesh* was an undertaker in Jenkintown, Pennsylvania. *Joseph St. Peter* was a morgue attendant in Washington D.C. *John Wellbeloved* sued for divorce in Georgia. *Penny Cash* worked for the I.R.S. in Wyoming. *T. Hee* was a gag writer for Disney films. *Hans Hoff* was a psychiatrist in Vienna. *Mr. Lawless* was elected judge in Pasco, Washington. *John Minor Wisdom* was a federal judge in New Orleans. *Dr. Stasick* was a physician in Hammond, Indiana. *Mr. S. Hoving* was a moving contractor. *J. E. Weller* was a jeweller. *F. E. Male* was male. More authentic names: *Mrs. L. E. Fant, C. Wilbert Wiggle, Frank D. Press, Dr. I. N. King, B. A. Handshaker.* A man named *I. Will Love* was 80 years old when he battled a 46-year-old rival for the hand of a 40-year old woman. In 1962 *Professor Harvard, Professor Cornell,* and *Professor Yale* all taught at Yale University. Walter Sippey of Zaneville, Ohio, had a wife who was of course *Mrs. Sippey.* Syngman Rhee, former president of the Republic of Korea, would be known as *Mr. Rhee* in the U.S.— a real enigma.

Son Of A...

In Polish, the suffix '-ski' means son of. The suffix 'a' means daughter of. Therefore, Madame Curie's maiden name was Sklodowska, but her brother's name was Jozef Sklodowski. This system of naming was adopted about 600 years ago in Poland, and by the year 1500, 75% of Polish names ended in '-ski.' In Russian, the suffixes '-ov' and '-ev' denote who you're the son of, as in Khrushchev, Molotov, and Brezhnev. About 70% of all Russian names end in one of these two ways. In Spanish '-ez' also means son of: Fernandez, Gonzalez, Martinez. In Swedish, '-sen' or '-son' means son of. The ten most common Swedish surnames are Andersson, Johansson, Karlsson, Nilsson, Eriksson, Larsson, Olsson, Pettersson, Svensson, and Persson. In 1900, 60% of the Danish population had names that ended in '-sen.' Legislation passed in 1904 asked people to adopt other, more different names. In Welsh, 'ap' means son of. Ap Rhys was Americanized to Price; ap Richard became Prichard; ap John became Upjohn; ap Harry became Parry; and ap Howell became Powell. In Greek, '-poulos' is the suffix that means son of, as in Papadhopoulos, meaning 'son of the priest.' The 'O' prefix in Irish names as in O'Brien means 'descended from,' and the prefix 'Mac' as in MacDonald means son. 'Mac' was often abbreviated as 'Mc.' Jews in eastern Europe used 'ben' to denote paternity. David ben Gurion was the son of Gurion. German and Austrian Jews used the ending '-sohn,' as in Mendelsohn.

Misc. Bits

- During the 1700s in Germany, all Jews were required by law to adopt a last name. For a large fee, they could buy a nice name like Rosenthal, meaning rose valley. Those who refused to pay were given ugly names like Schmalz, meaning grease, or Eselkopf, meaning donkey head.

—Names—

- A law prohibits anyone from using the name of any living person in ads or literature without getting their permission. Groucho Marx thought he was playing it safe when he invented the name Brindlebug, but a Mr. Brindlebug appeared to protest the use of his name. A real Ichabod Crane protested Washington Irving's use of his name. Charlie Chaplin used the name Henri Verdoux in the film *Monsieur Verdoux* after searching phone books to make sure no one by that name was listed. Still, a real Mr. Verdoux showed up and sued.
- William Stanislaus Murphy willed his fortune to Harvard University on the condition that they use the money to provide scholarships for people named Murphy. Likewise, John Nicholson of London in 1717 willed his money for the use of poor protestant people in England who were named Nicholson.
- A survey taken in the U.S. in 1790 showed that 91.8% of names used were British in origin. German names accounted for 5.6%, and Dutch names comprised 2%. All other nationalities made up for 1% of the names.
- Willie Barkley maintained that no one could go far in life with the name Willie. He insisted people call him by his middle name, Alben. Alben Barkley became vice-president under Harry Truman.
- Lincoln married a woman named Mary Todd. When asked how to spell his wife's maiden name, with one D or two, Lincoln replied, "One D is enough for God, but the Todds need two."

Name Change

- In 1955 New Orleans police picked up a man on a minor charge. They became suspicious when he gave his name as Davy Crockett. A fingerprint check revealed him to be a criminal whose given name was actually Daniel Boone.
- Elias Harlampopoulas was a Chicago meat dealer who changed his name to Louis Harris. He was back in court a little later asking to have his original name reinstated. He explained that most of his customers were Greek and they could not pronounce Harris.
- Edward Looney of New Haven, Connecticut, changed his name to Lowney because he planned on becoming a psychiatrist.
- Richard Rotten changed his name to Wroughton.
- Mahran Gouzoukouchokian of Elizabeth, New Jersey, changed his name to Mahron Levon because too many people were saying "Gesundheit" after he introduced himself.
- Allan Haines Lockheed, the aircraft engineer, was named Loughead but changed his name because people kept calling him Loghead.
- Otto Hell changed his name to Hall because people called him O. Hell.
- Wlodzimierz Roger Leliwa-Tyskiewicz changed his name to Wlodzimierz Roger Tyszkiewicz because it was less complicated.
- Edward L. Hayes of San Francisco felt that Hayes was a name that had no future potential for him, so he changed his name to Tharnmidsbe Lurgy Praghustspondgifcem. He later decided that name wasn't good enough either,

so he tried to change his name to Miswaldpornghuestficset Balstemdrigneshoiwintpluaslof Wradvaistplondqueskycrufemglish. The judge decided that was too much and refused.

Alias

About 75% of actors and actresses have adopted new names. Liberace was Wladziu Valentino. Lucille Ball was Diane Belmont. Ginger Rogers was Virginia McMath. Kirk Douglas was Issur Danielovitch. Cyd Charisse was Tula Ellice Finklea. Joan Crawford was Lucille Le Sueur. Boris Karloff was William Henry Pratt. Zsa Zsa Gabor was Sari Gabor. The Marx brothers were playing poker one night with a talent agent who suggested that Julius, Adolph, Herbert, Leonard, and Milton Marx change their names to Groucho, Harpo, Zeppo, Chico, and Gummo.

You Said A Mouthful

- Perhaps the longest legitimate last name was Lambros Pappatorianofillosopoulos of Chicopee, Massachusetts. He was inducted into the Army in 1953. People called him simply Pappas, or Mr. Alphabet.
- George Pappavlahodimitrakopoulous owned a restaurant in Lansing, Michigan in 1961. He said he'd give a free meal to anyone who could pronounce his name correctly.
- Paul Panagiotopoulos of St. Paul was once asked why he didn't shorten his name. He replied that he did shorten his name— it used to be Apostolopanagiotopoulos.
- Spiro Agnew shortened his real name of Anagnostopoulos.

The Final Fact

In its issue of Feb. 16, 1962, *Time* magazine printed a letter to the editor that criticized diplomat Krishna Menon. It was signed by four Hindus. The following week they published a letter from a man at Columbia University who pointed out that the four "signatures" were not names at all, but four vulgar obscenities in the Hindu language.

ZANY 'Z' FACTS

The First Fact

When the film *Razzamatazz* was finished, a studio boss called the producers to his office and angrily demanded, "Which one of you smart guys figured there was a theater owner in the country who had four Zs in his marquee letters?" The name of the movie was quickly changed.

An Unusual Holiday

January 1st is National "Z" Day, whose purpose is to give recognition on the first day of the year to all persons and places whose name begins with the letter Z and are always listed or thought of last. For instance, there's the zorilla, which is the world's smelliest animal. It looks like a cross between a weasel, badger, and skunk, and it lives in Africa. It's a carnivorous animal that eats rats, snakes, and insects. It can discharge a fluid that can be detected for a half mile radius and smells so horrible it will keep full grown lions at bay. Let us also remember Frank Zarb, who in 1975 spent $25,000 and used 19,000 gallons of fuel flying around the country to lecture on the need to conserve energy. He used a plush Air Force jet that burned enough fuel in one hour to supply the average American driver with enough gasoline to drive for an entire year. Then there was Mr. T. M. Zink, who died and left his fortune to fund a womanless library. Signs reading "No Women Admitted" were to be posted above the doors, and no books or art by women was to be allowed. Fortunately, Zink's family successfully contested the will.

Ziegler, Zenger, Zeno Etc.

- In 1974 the Doublespeak Award for outrageous language went to Ron Ziegler, Nixon's press secretary. When asked whether Watergate tapes were still intact— a question that could have been answered with yes, no, or I don't know— Ziegler used a colossal 99-word sentence that left everybody wondering if the answer was yes, no, or I don't know. Zielger said, "If my answers sound confusing, I think they are confusing because the questions are confusing, and the situation is confusing and I'm not in a position to clarify it."
- In 1733 dentures gave rise to an important legal test case. John Zenger, editor of the *New York Weekly Journal,* said about Governor William Cosby that he had loathsome false teeth and an unclean mouth. The Governor sued for libel. Zenger's lawyer maintained the comments were not libelous unless it could be proven that the comments were wrong. The jury must have agreed that the Governor had loathsome false teeth, because they found Zenger not guilty.
- In 264 B.C. Greek philosopher Zeno suffered a broken toe and decided this was God's sign that he had lived long enough. He killed himself, dying at age 98.
- Florenze Ziegfeld of the Ziegfeld Follies once offered Gracie Allen $750 a week to appear in a London show. Gracie asked how much the pay would be if her husband, George Burns, appeared too. "Five hundred," was the answer.

Zuider Zee

The Netherlands were fighting Spain during the winter of 1573. The fiord called Zuider Zee froze over and the Spanish ships were trapped in the ice. The Netherlanders waited until the ice was thick enough, then rode out to the ships on horseback and captured them— the only known instance when a naval battle was won on horseback.

Zoysia

Specialists at the U.S. Department of Agriculture have been experimenting with a lawn that needs less watering and only a third as much mowing as regular lawns. The key is a type of grass called zoysia. It grows sideways along the ground instead of up, so it needs less mowing. It tolerates drought, so it needs less watering. Equally promising is a mixture of zoysia and fescue that can stay green year-round in the south. The zoysia is green in the summer and the fescue is green in the winter. Also in the works is tougher turf for football and baseball fields.

Zoo Facts

- A male orangutan at the Henry Doorly Zoo in Omaha, Nebraska confounded keepers for weeks. At night he would be locked safely inside his cage, yet the next morning workers would find him roaming freely through the corridors behind the exhibits. Every night security was double checked, and every morning the animal would be found loose. Finally it was discovered that the orangutan had a small piece of wire, which he kept hidden in his mouth. At night he would use it to pick the lock on his cage, and gain the reward of freedom.
- A chimp in a zoo was once having trouble with a loose baby tooth that wouldn't come out. Some of its comrades tried to pull the tooth, but they couldn't get a good grip on it. Finally an attendant handed the chimps a pair of pliers. In only a few moments, they figured out what pliers were for and the tooth was out.
- In 1981 at the San Diego Zoo an elephant named Lucy came down with a toothache and lost nearly 700 pounds because she couldn't chew. A veterinary dentist sedated her and removed the five-pound molar with an electric drill, a crowbar, and a sledgehammer.

- Paintings hung in a London art gallery received critical acclaim. The modern artist who had done the paintings was known only as Congo. Critics noted that the art was well-composed and colorful. Finally it was revealed that Congo was a chimp living in the London Zoo.
- At the Bronx Zoo gift shop you can buy paintings done by the chimps.
- In an experiment in 1962, researchers recorded the sounds baboons made in the wild while storm clouds were gathering. Later the tape was played to captive apes in a zoo. Even though the day was perfectly clear, the apes rushed to shelter as if a storm had been imminent.
- The San Diego Zoo breeds roaches to feed their bird collection. They are high in vitamin B.
- Jody Sussman and Kurt Metzger got married in front of the gorilla house at the Cincinnati Zoo. If it had rained they had alternate plans to marry in the bird house. They said they both loved animals and wanted to be married in the place that meant the most to them.
- An ostrich at the Hanover Zoo bent a quarter-inch iron bar into a right angle with a single kick.
- In 1904 a pygmy from Africa was brought to the St. Louis Expo to appear in a freak show. His name was Ota Benga. Whether he had been kidnapped from Africa or whether he came of his own volition is not known. After the Expo was over, he was donated to the Bronx Zoo. His teeth were filed to a point to make a better pygmy-type presentation and he was displayed in a cage as a cannibal. An orangutan and a parrot were his companions. The spectacle caused quite a lot of controversy and the zoo was threatened with legal action. They released the man from his cage and he was free to stroll the zoo grounds, where he was regularly followed by curious crowds. Later he was sent to college and went to live with a Virginia family. He committed suicide in 1916.
- An attendant at the zoo in Prague got some bad stains on his shirt in 1982. He sent the dirty shirt to the laundry, but when it came back the stains were still visible. He wore the shirt to work anyway. Then one hot day he removed it and laid it aside. An elephant snatched it up and gulped it down before he could do anything. When the shirt reappeared at the opposite end of the elephant a few days later, it was still intact— and the stains were gone.
- An artist at the Memphis Zoo decided to decorate the zoo walls with murals of African scenery. His paintings were perhaps a little too lifelike, as numerous birds tried to fly into the wild blue yonder.

Quips & Quotes

"A zoo is a place of refuge where savage beasts are protected from people."
-Gerald Lieberman

"Zoo: an excellent place to study the habits of human beings." *-Evan Esar*

"When I was a kid I said to my father one afternoon, 'Daddy, will you take me to the zoo?' He answered, 'If the zoo wants you, let them come and get you.'"
-Jerry Lewis

Zoo Jokes

- Visitors at a zoo were amazed to see a cage labeled "Peaceful Co-Existence" which held a fox and several chickens. The zoo keeper said it was easy to maintain the arrangement; all they had to do was occasionally toss in a few more chickens.
- A huge elephant and a tiny mouse were in the same cage. The elephant looked down at the mouse and said in disgust, "You're the puniest, weakest, most insignificant thing I've ever seen!" "Well," replied the mouse, "Don't forget—I've been sick!"
- There was a big fight in the lion house. One lion called another a cheetah.
- Two monkeys discussing evolution: "You mean to tell me that I'm my keeper's brother?"
- Male elephant as female elephant passes: "Wow! A perfect 258-297-314!"
- One elephant to the other: "I'm getting sick and tired of working for peanuts!"

Story

The story goes that Greek painters Zeuxis and Parrhasius had a feud concerning who could produce the most realistic painting. Finally they agreed to a paint-off. Zeuxis painted a picture of a boy holding a bowl of grapes. It was so realistically done that birds came down to peck at the picture. Then Zeuxis asked Parrhasius to draw back the curtain covering the painting he had drawn.  At this point Zeuxis realized that what he thought was a curtain covering a painting was actually a painting of a curtain covering a painting. Zeuxis had been able to fool the birds, but Parrhasius had been able to fool Zeuxis.

Misc. Z Bits

- The ZIP code stands for Zoning Improvement Plan. Zip codes began in 1963.
- The postman in Zurs, Austria, was overtaken by an avalanche. His dog walked over the snow and stationed himself at a particular spot, refusing to move for three days. Villagers finally decided to dig where the dog sat, and found the postmaster still alive.
- An estimated 20% of Zambia's adult urban population is infected with the AIDS virus.
- Zucchini is one of the least caloric foods.
- In Romania, the new mayor of the town of Zimnicea took the oath of office minutes before a serious earthquake hit in 1977. Instead of celebrating political victory, he was dealing with disaster on his first day in office.
- After Mt. St. Helens erupted, people mailrd envelopes full of ash to relatives, but they kept breaking open and ruining the post office's sorting machines. The postmaster requested people to enclose the ash in zip-lock baggies.

Zany Z Facts

- When Zeus wanted to have an affair, he convinced a nymph named Echo to divert his wife's attention by conversing with her. When his wife found out about it, she confiscated Echo's ability to talk and sentenced her to forever repeat the last words of whatever she heard.
- Leonard Nimoy played a zombie in *Zombies of the Stratosphere.*
- Zeppo Marx invented a wristwatch that monitors the wearer's heartbeat and sounds an alarm if it is abnormal.
- Pearl Grey was the world's foremost western novelist. Before becoming an author, however, a name change was in order. He changed his name to Zane Grey. Zane Grey was a dentist before he was a writer.
- British novelist Israel Zangwill once received a letter from his friend, Andrew Lang, asking whether or not he was going to attend a local event. Zangwill's reply was, "If you, Lang, will, I. Zangwill."
- The world's largest zipper is in the Houston Astrodome, zipping the turf together.
- The government's term for zipper is 'interlocking slide fastener.'

Quote

"A dress that zips up the back will bring a husband and wife together."

-James Boren

A Penny Saved...

A computer programmer working for a large bank wrote instructions to the mainframe directing it to deduct the odd cents below ten cents from every current account at the end of each month and credit it to the last account on record. The programmer then opened an account for himself under the assumed name of Mr. Zyglit. Things went fine for six months. Then a Polish immigrant legitimately named Mr. Zyzov opened a new account. When he went to the bank to ask them why so much money was being deposited in his account, an investigation was launched and the programmer arrested.

Z Quotes

"Mass media do more to keep Americans stupid than even the whole U.S. school system." *-Frank Zappa*

"There are too many people, and not enough human beings." *-Robert Zend*

"People have one thing in common: they are all different." *-Robert Zend*

"Being a philosopher, I have a problem for every solution." *-Robert Zend*

"He is either dead or teaching school." *-Zenobius* (1st Century)

"Criticism comes easier than craftsmanship." *-Zeuxis*

"What I want to do is to make people laugh so that they'll see things seriously." *-Wm. Zinsser*

"The only way to stop smoking is to just stop— no ifs, ands, or butts." *-Edith Zittler*

"Perfection is such a nuisance that I often regret having cured myself of using tobacco." *-Émile Zola*

"Coward: A man in whom the instinct of self-preservation acts normally."
-Sultana Zoraya

"Nothing can take the place of practical experience out in the world."
-A. B. Zu Tavern

Zinnias

According to the story, a German botanist was exploring Mexico, looking for new specimens. When he found a beautiful purple flower, he gathered a sack full of the seed heads. Suddenly he was seized by bandits who thought his sack must be full of gold. When they opened it and found only a bunch of dead flowers, the robbers were convinced the botanist was an idiot, wandering through the desert with a bunch of faded flowers. Because it was considered bad luck to murder the feeble-minded, the bandits let the man go. The flowers he was collecting were taken back to Europe and examined by another botanist named Dr. Johann Gottfried Zinn. Dr. Zinn named them after himself: zinnias.

The Final Fact

An entomologist who had just discovered a new species of moth was determined to have the final word. He invented a name for the insect that guaranteed it the final spot in every dictionary in the world: Zyzzyx.

OLD AGE

The First Fact

The oldest authenticated age of a human was a Japanese man who died in 1985 at the age of 120.

Animal Ages

- The oldest dinosaurs probably lived to about the age of 200. Humans live a maximum of 115 years and an average of 71, one the longest lifespans in the animal world. The elephant can live a maximum of 77 years; the horse can live 62 years; the donkey 50 years; the hippo 49; the rhino 45; and the chimp 39.
- The oldest chicken known was 14 years old. Chickens normally live about seven years.
- One pigeon was known to have lived 39 years.
- The average American baby can expect to live 78.3 years if it's female, or 71.0 years if male. That's a full 20 years more than the average Pakistani man who can expect to live only 51.0 years.

Lifespans

Researcher Jay Gould studied different animals and calculated the ratio of each animal's breath rate, heart rate, body weight and lifespan. He discovered a consistent ratio: if you multiply the pace of the animal's biological ticking by its lifespan, the number that results is virtually constant. Gould concluded each animal lives for about the same amount of "biological time." A tiny mouse with a fast heartbeat, quick digestion, and frantic scurrying will live for about the same amount of heartbeats as the large and sedate grizzly bear, which has a slow heartbeat, a sluggish digestive tract, and a ponderous manner. One exception to the rule is the human being, who lives three times as long as size and internal speed would indicate. We live about 48 years longer than the ratio predicts. Another exception concerns dogs. Large dogs generally have a shorter lifespan than smaller ones. Great Danes seldom live longer than 10 years, but poodles frequently live past 15 years of age.

In one experiment, Gould forced the metabolism of mice to slow down by feeding them less. They lived three times longer than normal mice.

Fact

Professional people such as doctors and lawyers have the longest lifespans, followed by administrators and managers, then farmers and skilled laborers, followed by unskilled laborers.

Good News

A study done by the Stanford University School of Medicine has recently reconfirmed what we should know already. Running is good for your health. The subject of the study was runners over the age of 50. Participants in the study ran an average of 27 miles per week and had been running for an average of 11 years. Among the results: Female runners were sick for an average of two days per year compared to 11 sick days for nonrunners. Male runners missed an average of 1.5 days of work each year due to illness, whereas male nonrunners missed an average of 4.4 days. Runners visited their doctors an average of 2.1 times per year, compared to 2.6 times for nonrunners. However, one-third of those visits were for running-related injuries. Runners had lower heart rates and blood pressure than nonrunners and weighed an average of 15 pounds less than nonrunners.

Bad News

- Cardiovascular problems are responsible for more than half the deaths of people over the age of 65.
- Adults lose muscle tissue at the rate of .44% per year. Between the ages of 20 and 70, 25% of the original muscle mass is replaced by fat.
- Vision peaks at the age of 17. Only one out of every eight 80-year-olds has 20/20 vision.
- The brain loses about three ounces of weight by the age of 80. The brain loses cells at the rate of 50,000 per day by the age of 30.
- The strength of a man's biceps is halved between the age of 25 and 60.
- The heart of a 70-year-old man pumps a quart less blood per minute than it did 40 years earlier.
- A 70-year-old man will inhale half as much air as he did at age 20, and will have only one-third the number of taste buds on the tongue. This sometimes leads to oversalting, which exacerbates the problems of high blood pressure.
- 10% of people over 65 suffer from Alzheimer's disease and other forms of senile dementia.
- 67% of people who have ever lived beyond age 65 are alive today.
- 78% of doctors surveyed by the American Medical Association said they favor turning off life-support systems in hopeless cases when urged to do so by the

patients or their families.
- Cells taken from a fetus and placed in a nutritive solution will divide about 50 times before dying. Cells taken from an old person divide only two to ten times before dying.
- Memory begins to decline around the age of 30. When given a list of 24 words to memorize, a 20-year-old will recall an average of 14; a 40-year-old will recall 11; at 60 only nine words are remembered; and at 70 only seven. However, vocabulary is three times as great by age 45 as at age 22; and by 60 the brain contains four times as much information as it did at age 21.
- In general a newborn sleeps an average of 20 hours a day; a 1-year-old, 13 hours; 16-year-old, nine hours; a 40-year-old, seven hours; a 50-year-old, five hours.
- Hearing is fully developed by age seven and deteriorates from there. Children are able to hear sounds up to 40,000 vibrations per second, but by age 16 it's down to 20,000 per second and it continues to drop by about 80 vibrations per second every six months after that. Frequent exposure to loud noise accelerates the decline. This was proven in a study done of the Mabaan tribe in the Sudan. They use neither guns nor drums; they always speak in whispers and never shout; and the loudest thing they are ever exposed to is a clap of thunder or the roar of a lion. Their hearing, when tested, proved to be better than any human hearing ever examined because their inner ear cells were spared all trauma.
- The suicide rate for those age 75 and older is twice the rate of the young. People over 60 represent 12% of the U.S. population, but are responsible for 25% of the suicides.

Quips & Quotes

"Inside every older person, there's a younger person, wondering what happened." *-Ashleigh Brilliant*

"If you laugh a lot, when you get older your wrinkles will be in the right places." *-Andrew V. Mason, M.D.*

"A young boy is a theory; an old man is a fact." *-Ed Howe*

"I smoke cigars because at my age if I don't have something to hold onto, I might fall down." *-George Burns*

"The hardest years in life are those between 10 and 70." *-Helena Hayes at age 83*

"After age 70 it's patch, patch, patch." *-Jimmy Stewart*

"The secret of staying young is to live honestly, eat slowly, and lie about your age." *-Lucille Ball*

"If there were 15 months in every year, I'd only be 48." *-James Thurber at age 65*

"When a man retires and time is no longer a matter of urgent importance, his colleagues generally present him with a watch." *-R.C. Sherriff*

"If I'd known I was going to live so long, I'd have taken better care of myself." *-Leon Eldred*

Old Age

"Methuselah lived to be 969 years old. You boys and girls will see more in the next 50 years than Methuselah saw in his whole lifetime."   *-Mark Twain*

"You know you're getting old when the candles cost more than the cake."

-Bob Hope

Wit Bits

- German statesman Konrad Adenauer was nearly 90 years old when he went to see his doctor about a heavy cold. He was impatient and demanding, and the offended doctor said, "I'm not a magician. I can't make you young again!" Adenauer replied, "I haven't asked you to— all I want is to go on getting older!"

- Actress Ethel Barrymore was in her dressing room when an usher knocked on the door and announced, "There's a couple ladies in the reception room who say they went to school with you. What shall I do with them?" Ethyl replied, "Wheel them in!"

- Actor John Barrymore was attending a funeral and was about to leave when he saw a very old man looking at the grave. Barrymore went over to him and said, "I guess it hardly pays to go home."

- When John Barrymore was getting on in years, someone asked him if acting was still as fun as it used to be. He answered, "Young man, I am 75. Nothing is as much fun as it used to be."

- When he was 80 years old, Roman statesman Cato decided to start studying Greek. When his friends expressed surprise that he was beginning such a lengthy study at such an advanced age, he replied that this was the youngest age he had left.

- Chevalier was 73 years old when a group of pretty showgirls walked past. He heaved a sigh and said, "Ah, if only I were 20 years older!" "Don't you mean 20 years younger?" responded his companion. "No," Chavalier explained. "If I were 20 years older, then these girls would not bother me the way they do now."

- A photographer was taking Winston Churchill's picture on Churchill's 80th birthday. The photographer said he hoped he would have the honor of photographing Churchill on his 100th birthday as well. "I don't see why not,"

—Old Age—

replied Churchill. "You look reasonably fit to me."
- French writer Alexandre Dumas was once asked how he managed to grow old so gracefully. He replied, "I devote all my time to it."
- Casey Stengel was in his 70s when someone asked him how he was doing. "Not bad," he answered. "Most of the people my age are dead."
- French conductor Pierre Monteax was being interviewed on his 89th birthday. He was asked what he enjoyed in life. He replied, "I still have two abiding passions. One is my model railway, the other — women. But at the age of 89, I find I am getting just a little too old for model railways."
- Austrian economist Ludwig VonMises was asked, at the age of 88, how he felt when he woke up in the morning. "Amazed," he said.
- Novelist W. Somerset Maugham was being honored at a dinner party on his 80th birthday. He rose to give a speech, saying, "There are many virtues in growing old..." He paused, looking at the ground, thinking hard. The audience began to fidget. He shuffled his notes. People began to look uneasy. He shifted from foot to foot. People exchanged embarrassed glances. Finally he continued, "I was just trying to think what they are."
- French writer Bernard de Fontenelle was quite old when an equally elderly friend of his said, "Death has forgotten us." Fontenelle replied, "SHHH!"

Old Marriages

- Moses Alexander, aged 93, married Mrs. Frances Tompkins, aged 105, in Bata, New York, on June 11, 1831. They were both found dead in bed the following morning.
- In 1984 in Milwaukee, Ida Stern, age 91, divorced her husband Simon, age 97.
- Octavio Guillen and Adriana Martinez were engaged for 67 years before finally getting married in Mexico City in 1969. They were both 82 years old.
- Lazarus Rowe was 18 years old when he wed Molly Webber in 1743. He died in 1829, ending a marriage lasting 86 years.

Wit Bits

- "To what do you attribute your long life?" asked a reporter of the 100-year-old man on his birthday. "It's simple," replied the old man. "I've been taking vitamins since my 99th birthday!"
- Gravestone in Novia Scotia: "Here lies Ezekiel Ailke, Age 102. The Good Die Young."

Antics & Anecdotes

- Rep. Emanuel Celler was the oldest person in the House of Representatives. He was speaking in favor of a measure when he forgot some facts and had to be reminded. "You know, there are three signs of aging. The first is that you tend to forget things rather easily— and for the life of me, I don't know what the other two things are."
- Visiting a small English town, Prince Phillip stopped to chat with two very old women. "I'm 104," said one of the ladies, "and my friend here is 101." "I don't believe you," replied Phillip. "Ladies always take ten years off their age."

- British aristocrat Lord William Alvanley was involved in a fender-bender when his horse-drawn coach ran into another. The owner of the other coach jumped out, ready to thrash Alvanley's careless coachman. When he saw the coachman was a small, elderly man, he cried, "Your age protects you!" Lord Alvanley had jumped from his coach ready to beat the other man, but seeing that it was a large young man, he replied, "Your youth protects *you*!" and got back into his coach.
- When George Burns reached the age of 85, he remarked, "I was always taught to respect my elders and I've now reached the age when I don't have anybody to respect."
- On Cary Grant's birthday, a reporter sent him a cable saying, "How old Cary Grant?" Grant wired back, "Old Cary Grant fine. How you?"

The Good News

At age 100 Grandma Moses was painting. At 93 George Bernard Shaw wrote the play *Farfetched Fables*. At 90 Pablo Picasso was still drawing. At 89 Arthur Rubinstein gave one of his greatest recitals at Carnegie Hall. At 88 Michelangelo was doing architectural plans. At 82 Winston Churchill wrote *A History of the English-Speaking Peoples*. At 81 Benjamin Franklin made the compromise that led to the adoption of the Constitution. At 82 Leo Tolstoy wrote *I Cannot Be Silent*. At 81 Goethe finished *Faust*. At 80 George Burns won an Academy Award for *The Sunshine Boys*. In 1965 Leroy Paige pitched three scoreless innings for the Kansas City Athletics at the age of 59 to become the oldest major leaguer. Sarah Bernhardt portrayed Juliet in Shakespeare's *Romeo and Juliet* when she was 70.

The Final Fact

50% of Americans polled said they would like to live to be 100.

HUMOR

The First Fact

Abbott & Costello took out a $100,000 insurance policy with Lloyds of London that would pay off should any audience members die of laughter.

Antics & Anecdotes

- The head of the Coca-Cola company, Bob Woodruff, once went turkey hunting with ventriloquist Edgar Bergen. Both of them saw a turkey and fired at it simultaneously. The turkey fell dead, but they each insisted they had been the one to shoot the bird. Finally Bergen claimed, "There's only one way to settle this." He picked up the bird, propped it up on his knee, and asked, "Who shot you, bird?" The turkey answered, "You did, Bergen."
- Ethel Merman was dining at an open air cafe in New York. Her small dog was tied up at her feet, begging for scraps. She was having a salad and had nothing to give him. Finally a man dining near her got up and left his table, leaving a large tasty piece of lambchop on his plate. She couldn't resist— she slipped the chop off his plate and snuck it to her dog under the table. A few minutes later the man returned to his table. He had gone to use the telephone and was very perplexed to find his lunch missing.
- Sir Thomas Beecham was conducting an orchestra rehearsal when he complained that the first trombonist was playing his part much too loudly. The other players pointed out the trombonist was late for rehearsal and had not even arrived yet. "Very well, then, when he *does* arrive, tell him he is playing too loudly."
- While John Barrymore was suffering through his final illness, his doctor prescribed a sparse diet and ordered him to do very little. After eating his tiny little meal, the nurse asked him if she could do anything for him. He responded, "Yes, could you get me a postage stamp? I believe I'll do a little reading."
- Once poet Edwin Arlington Robinson was asked by an aspiring writer, "What is the most important qualification for a beginner in poetry?" Robinson answered, "A small appetite."
- Fanny Brice once remarked, "I owe my success to the peaceful home life I enjoyed as a child. Anything my mother wanted to do, Pop let her do, saying she had a perfect right... She had a pretty good left, too."
- When Bob Hope quipped, "My hotel room is so small that the rats are stoop-shouldered" the hotel threatened to sue unless he took it back. So in his next routine, he quipped, "I'm sorry I said that the rats in that hotel were stoop-shouldered. They are not."
- Adelaide Hawley, alias Betty Crocker, received a letter from a woman who needed special high-altitude cooking instructions immediately, because she was moving from the 4th floor of a high-rise apartment building to the 23rd.
- Woodrow Wilson was asked how long it took him to prepare a ten-minute speech. "Two weeks," was the answer. And how long did it take him to prepare

a one-hour speech? "One week." And how long to prepare a two-hour speech? "I am ready now!"
- Jean Kerr wrote *Please Don't Eat the Daisies* in which she told humorous stories about the problems of raising four boys. One of her young sons had to write a book report, so he of course chose to review his mother's book. He concluded the report by saying, "Mrs. Kerr has written a very funny book, although the parts about her children are greatly exaggerated and in some instances are downright lies."

Quick Quips

- Even if your dreams haven't come true, be thankful that your nightmares haven't come true either.
- Many things have been blamed on the stork which should have been blamed on the lark.
- If it weren't for the last minute, nothing would ever get done.
- Bad spellers of the world, UNTIE!
- It's easy to make a friend. It's harder to make a stranger.
- The wages of sin are unreported.
- A friend in need is a friend to dodge.

Robert Benchley

- Robert Benchley was one of America's finest humorists. He loved practical jokes. While in college, he and a friend were walking through the richest section in Boston when Benchley exclaimed, "Come on, let's get the davenport." Knocking on the front door of a house picked at random, Benchley told the maid who answered, "We're here to fetch the davenport." The flustered maid asked which davenport he meant. He pointed to a couch inside the door. She let them in and the two men carried the couch away. They took it across the street, where they knocked on another door. When the maid answered, Benchley said, "We're here to deliver the davenport. Where shall we put it?" She showed them

—Humor—

to the sitting room, where they deposited it and left.
- While walking by Ulysses S. Grant's tomb, Benchley scribbled something on a slip of paper and stuck it under the monument. The note said, "Please leave two quarts Grade A and a pint whipping cream. -U.S.G."
- Benchley was drinking with Dorothy Parker in a speakeasy when they were approached by a man who offered to sell them a watch reputed to be indestructible. Benchley and Parker tested it by banging it against the bar, throwing it on the floor, and stomping on it. The salesman picked it up, listened to it, and announced it was no longer ticking. "Maybe you wound it too tight," Benchley and Parker replied in unison.
- Benchley and Parker shared an office that was so small Benchley remarked, "One cubic foot less of space and it would have constituted adultery."
- Benchley was amazed when his request for a bank loan was granted unconditionally. He immediately closed his account, saying, "I don't trust a bank that would lend money to such a poor risk!"

Bloopers

- From a Michigan paper: "Rudy Menzel just returned from Canada with a 1,300 pound mouse. This was Rudy's first hunting experience with big game."
- From the Fort Worth *Press*: "Studies of male-type baldness indicate that one-fourth of all men will show some baldness at age 25 and about half of them will exhibit some boldness by the age of 50."
- From the El Paso *Times*: "Mr. Brown has grown in stature through the ears."
- From the Cheney, Washington *Free Press*: "Eight candidates, including all four incompetents, are seeking the four City Council positions."
- From a political ad: "Floyd Cavanaugh— Justice of Peace. A Tired and True Democrat."
- During a typhoid epidemic in Germany, U.S. Army officials circulated orders that stated: "All ice cubes will be boiled before using."
- In a church bulletin: "'Spiritual Growth' will be postponed until September."
- In a West Virginia paper: "'Change Your Wife Through Prayer' will be the sermon subject Sunday."
- From the Tuscaloosa, Alabama *News*: "The Skyland Garden Club will meet Thursday at 10 a.m. at the country club. Shady subjects will be discussed."
- In a California newspaper: "Many Antiques at D.A.R. Meeting."
- From the Hartford, Connecticut *Times*: "Representatives from 14 of the town's package stores met last night to hear some advice about how they can protect themselves from Police Chief Herman O. Schendel."
- Classified in the Seattle *Times*: "Girl wanted to hell with the washing and ironing."
- An ad for a dry cleaner: "Get them in Friday. We will have them black Saturday."

Wit Bits

- Man with a new library card: "With this card I can take out any book?"

Librarian: "Yes." Man: "And I may take out record albums, too?" Librarian: "Yes." Man: "And may I take *you* out?" Librarian: "The librarians are for reference only!"

- Jack: "How's things at home today?" Mack: "Well, the old woman ain't talking to me this morning, and I ain't in a mood to interrupt her."
- Judge: "Why don't you two men settle this dispute out of court?" Litigants: "That's what we were doing when the cops interfered!"
- Jud: "What's the first thing you notice about a girl?" Bud: "It depends on which way she's walking."
- Guest at a dude ranch: "I had no idea something filled with hay could ride so hard."
- Woman to best friend: "I went fishing with my husband today, and I did everything wrong. I talked too much, I used the wrong bait, I held the pole wrong, and I caught more than he did."

Richard Sheridan

- Richard Sheridan was an English playwright and member of Parliament. Once he came upon two of his friends. One of them said, "We have just been wondering whether you are a rogue or a fool." He stepped between them, took each one by the arm, and replied, "I believe I am between both."
- Sheridan was constantly in debt. One of his creditors asked him when he would pay up. "The day of judgement!" Sheridan cried. "No, wait—that will be a busy day. Make it the day after!"
- Another creditor asked Sheridan if he would at least pay the interest on his debt. He answered, "It is not my interest to pay the principal, nor my principle to pay the interest."
- Sheridan was once called on the carpet for having insulted a fellow member of Parliament. Forced to apologize, he wrote: "I said the honorable member was a liar it is true and I am sorry for it. The honorable member may place the punctuation where he pleases."
- Sheridan was manager of Drury Lane Theatre when it burned down in 1809. Watching the conflagration, Sheridan was apparently unruffled. A friend found him having a drink at a coffeehouse while he watched the fire, and remarked on how calm he was. "A man may surely be allowed to take a glass of wine by his own fireside," Sheridan replied.

Jokes Jokes Jokes

- Two friends discovered they were seeing the same psychiatrist. Both agreed he was too imperturbable and remained unruffled no matter what secrets. They agreed that at their next appointments, they'd each tell him what they had dreamed the previous night— and the dreams would be identical. They rehearsed the details of an outrageous dream. The next week, the first friend went in at 11 a.m. for his appointment and told the dream to the doctor. At 3 p.m. the second friend went in and also related his dream. "Funny thing about that dream," remarked the psychiatrist. "That's the third time I've heard it today."

—Humor—

- A Navy recruit lost his rifle. He was informed he'd have to pay to replace it. He asked, "If I were driving in a Navy jeep and someone stole it, would I have to pay for that, too?" The answer was yes, he'd have to pay for *any* government property he lost. "Now I understand why the captain always goes down with his ship."
- A young man needed to get some gas but found his wallet empty. Digging through his pockets he found some change. He pulled into the gas station and asked the attendant for a single gallon. The attendant asked, "What are you trying to do, wean it?"
- A fire inspector went to the roof of a skyscraper to check out fire hazards. The door slammed shut behind him, locking automatically. He was stranded. Hoping to get help, he started waving and jumping until he got the attention of a secretary in the window of a taller skyscraper next door. She just watched him disinterestedly. He tried pantomiming his plight, to no avail. Then he got an idea. Slowly he began stripping off his clothing, one piece at a time. By the time he removed his pants, the girl was reaching for a telephone. The building manager and police were there in a jiffy.
- A ship's captain insisted every square inch of the boat be kept in spotless condition. Sailors were kept constantly busy painting, scrubbing, and sweeping. Once he came across a sailor who was loafing around next to a newly painted door. "What are you doing, sitting there?" demanded the captain. "I'm just waiting for the paint to dry so I can start scrubbing it!"

Jimmy Durante

- At a race track, Jimmy Durante bet on a horse who lost by a nose. An ex-jocky nearby bragged, "What that horse needed was my riding." Durante retorted, "What he needed was my nose!"
- Durante once sang a duet on TV with opera diva Helen Traubel. The unlikely match-up was a tremendous success, and they later recorded the song. Traubel remarked, "It's a pleasure to record with a great artiste whose voice sounds the same with bad needles."
- After stepping into a crowded elevator on the way to the Starlight restaurant on top of the Waldorf Astoria, Durante was beseiged by fans wanting to shake his hand and offer compliments. "Folks! Folks!" he cried. "Save them adjectives— we got thoity floors to go!"

Quips & Quotes

- "The trouble with political promises is that they go in one year and out the other."
    -*Sylvia Bremer*

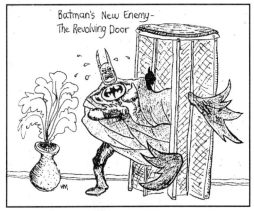

- "Men *do* make passes at girls who wear glasses. It depends on their frames."
  -Bob Sanders
- "My idea of a convincing talker is the fellow who can keep both hands in his pockets while describing the fish that got away." -Bob Hawk
- "Nobody ever forgets where he buried the hatchet." -Kin Hubbard
- "Worry: Interest paid on trouble before it falls due." -Dean Inge

Victor Borge

- In his early days as a comedian, Victor Borge was invited to perform at a supper club where he was told he would be paid $1 a head for every person who saw him perform. About 300 people showed up, but when the club's owner handed over $300, Victor pointed out that each of the club's 40 waiters also saw his performance. He got his extra $40.
- Victor Borge, after a show: "I wish to thank my mother and father, who made this show possible, and my five children, who made it necessary."
- Describing his childhood, he remarked, "Once my father came home and found me in front of a roaring fire. That made my father very mad, as we didn't have a fireplace."
- He quipped, "I only know two pieces. One is *Clair de Lune* and the other one isn't."
- Explaining why his piano keys were so yellow, Borge explained that it wasn't because his piano was so old. Rather, it was because the elephant smoked too much.

The Final Fact

Johnny Carson was asked what he wanted his epitaph to be. He replied, "I'll be right back!"

WAR

The First Fact
85% of casualties in armed conflicts since 1980 have been civilians.

Words Of War

- During the Revolutionary War, the American ship *Le Bonhomme Richard* was engaged in battle with the British *Serapis* off the coast of England. The *Richard* took a beating and was in danger of sinking. Her captain ordered his crew to close in, then lashed the two ships together. The captain of the *Serapis*, seeing the *Richard* begin to sink, asked for a surrender, but Captain John Paul Jones refused. History has filled in his words for him, "I have not yet begun to fight!" Locked together, the two ships mauled each other till the *Serapis* finally surrendered. The *Richard* sank soon after, but John Paul Jones sailed the *Serapis* home as a prize.

- Admiral David Farragut was leading the Union attack against the Confederates at Mobile Bay aboard the ironclad *Tecumseh*. The bay was heavily mined, forcing ships to pass dangerously close to the Confederate fort. The *Tecumseh* was sunk by a mine, so Farragut moved to the *Hartford* to continue the attack. The rest of the fleet was in disarray and the tide was sweeping them closer to the guns on shore. The Confederate ship *Tennessee* was closing in. Farragut called out, "Damn the torpedoes, go ahead!" The ships pressed on through the minefield without further damage. Soon both the fort and the *Tennessee* had fallen. Farragut's short but famous speech is now remembered as, "Damn the torpedoes, full speed ahead!"

- Chaplain Howell Forgy was aboard the cruiser *New Orleans* in Pearl Harbor when the Japanese attacked. The only man who had the keys that opened the ammunition room had gone ashore before the attack, so the crewmen were forced to break down the door. They were dismayed to find the automatic ammunition hoist was out of order. So the men formed a human chain to get the ammo on deck. Seeing the men tire after passing many heavy loads, Forgy called out, "Praise the Lord and pass the ammunition!" This later became the title of a popular song.

- During the War of 1812, the U.S. frigate *Chesapeake* was up against the British ship *Shannon* off the coast of Boston when the *Chesapeake's* captain, James Lawrence, was fatally wounded. His dying words were, "Don't give up the ship!"

- In 1813 during the Battle of Lake Erie, naval commander Oliver Hazard Perry was commanding the flagship *Lawrence* when it was so badly damaged that it was in danger of sinking. Perry had to row to a new ship to continue the battle. In spite of this, he won the battle. Later he sent a terse dispatch announcing victory, stating simply, "We have met the enemy, and they are ours." Years later Walt Kelly's cartoon character Pogo parodied this line by saying, "We have met the enemy and he is us."

The Cost Of War

- If all the money spent on military defense in the U.S. between the end of the Vietnam war and the beginning of the Iraqi war were refunded to Americans, each of us would receive $16,000.
- It would take 1/9th of the defense budget to lift every American over the poverty line for a year.
- Between 1981 and 1989 the military spent an average of $8,607 per *second*.
- The nations of the world spend over $10,000 per year training each soldier, but less than $100 per year educating each child.
- During World War II, it cost the U.S. an average of $225,000 to kill each enemy soldier.
- The world spends more than $1 billion a day on the military. That's $1 million every 90 seconds.
- A B-1 Stealth Bomber costs $400 million. If it were made of pure silver, it would only be worth 6% of its actual cost. The cost of flying a B-1 bomber for an hour is $21,000.
- In 1987 the Reagan administration budgeted $158,650,000 for the production of chemical weapons and $620,100,000 for the destruction of chemical weapons.
- In 1987 the Air Force spent $5,193,000 on imported goatskin jackets.
- You can buy 122 Cessna 172s for the price of one ground launched cruise missile.
- It's estimated that the U.S. defense uses about 10% of all the petroleum consumed in the U.S.

Strange Strategies

- In the 6th century B.C. the Persian army surrounded the Egyptian city of Memphis. Knowing that they thought of cats as sacred, the Persians began catapulting cats over the city walls. Horrified, the Egyptians surrendered rather than see more felines injured.
- When ancient Spain was invaded by armies of Pompey the Great, Spaniards abandoned their land, leaving behind them large tubs of honey. The invaders dug into the treat. Soon after, they all became deathly ill because of toxic impurities in the honey. The Spaniards, waiting in the hills nearby, returned to attack the disabled soldiers.

—War—

- When a bedbug senses human flesh, it makes an excited insect noise that might be called a miniature bark. During the Vietnam war, army scientists devised a plan whereby capsules containing bedbugs and tiny microphones would be dropped over suspected Vietcong hideouts. If a radio man heard the bugs barking, heavy artillery would be called in. Unfortunately, the war ended before this plan could be implemented.
- Stanley Lovell in his book *Of Spies and Stratagems* described a plot to foil the Nazis by waging glandular warfare against Hitler. Someone noticed that Hitler had strong female tendencies, and somebody else figured that if given female hormones, his voice would rise, his moustache fall out, and his appeal would plummet. So the OSS bribed Hitler's gardener to inject estrogen into his favorite vegetables. The plan failed, perhaps because the gardener kept the bribe and threw away the hormones.

The Full-figured Despot:

Kooky Causes

- In 1704 an Englishwoman spilled some wine on the Marquis de Torey of France. He thought she did it intentionally, and the insult ignited what turned out to be the War of the Spanish Succession, which rampaged through Europe for five years.
- In India in 1857 Hindu and Moslem soldiers served as British troops. When a rumor was spread that rifle cartridges were lubricated with pig grease and cow fat, mutiny ensued. The cartridges had to be uncapped in the mouth, violating their religious dietary laws against pork and beef. The resulting war was called the Sepoy Rebellion and is perhaps the only conflict caused by lard.

Fact

Since World War II, there has not been a single day when the world was free of war.

Food For Thought

- Aristotle told the story of the ancient city of Sybaris, where the horses were taught to dance to the music of a pipe. When the Sybarites went to war against the neighboring Crotonians, the Crotonians brought along a lot of pipes. On the battlefield, the pipers began to play, the Sybarian horses began to dance, and the riders were easily slaughtered.
- Rumors ran rampant in the ancient Greek city of Amyclae. Panic often ensued when false reports were spread of the approach of the Spartan army. Therefore, a law was passed forbidding such rumors, and death was the penalty for violation. When the Spartans really *did* march on the city, everyone was afraid

to report it. The city fell without a fight.
- The fight for independence was not unanimously supported in America. During the Revolutionary War, almost as many American colonists fought *for* the British as fought *against* them.
- When the first atomic bombs were dropped on Japan, no one knew about radiation sickness. Scientists thought the only people who would die from the bombs were those at ground zero. When the Japanese started complaining about the thousands who were dying of radiation, Americans thought it was propaganda designed to gain sympathy.
- When the German delegation requested armistice terms from the French at the end of World War II, they were presented with a set of conditions. "There must be some mistake," cried a German delegate. "These are terms which no civilized nation could impose on another!" "Glad to hear you say that," replied the French marshal. "These are not our terms. These are the terms imposed on the French town of Lille by the German commander when that city surrendered."
- During the Crimean War, a British officer was captured by the Russians. A search of his possessions revealed a letter from his sweetheart. In the letter she wrote that she was certain he would have good luck in his quest to capture Prince Menshikov and that he should be sure to send her one of his buttons as a souvenir. The letter was delivered to Prince Menshikov who found it so amusing that he removed a button and sent it to the officer with a note saying that although things had not taken place as the lady had wished, here was a button to present to her.
- During World War I, Captain J. H. Hedley was in a plane over Germany when the aircraft was hit. He was sucked out of the plane at 10,000 feet. The pilot of the plane took evasive action by plummeting in a vertical dive. When the plane pulled out of the dive, Hedley landed unhurt on the tail. He hung on until the plane was brought safely to a landing.
- In 1968 in L.A., former American fighter pilot Guy Harris announced he was offering for sale Adolf Hitler's toilet seat. He explained that he arrived at Hitler's headquarters just after the Russian troops cleaned the place out and pickings were pretty slim by the time he got there.

Another Fact
Suicide rates decrease during times of war.
Stupidity In War
- General John Sedgwick was inspecting troops during the Battle of the Wilderness in the Civil War. He had little respect for the enemy's ability to aim and stood gazing out over a parapet despite repeated warnings to duck down. He was shot dead.
- In 1893 British Vice Admiral Sir George Tryon was engaged in the battle of Tripoli when he ordered his ship to make a hard turn to port. His flag captain,

realizing that a turn to port would put the ship on a collision course with the attacking ship, guessed that the admiral had confused port with starboard. He queried the order. The admiral threatened to have him court-martialed if he didn't follow orders. The flag captain made the turn to port as required. The ship was rammed. Vice Admiral Sir George Tryon went down with his ship.

- On September 17, 1862, the Battle of Antietam took place when General Burnside ordered his Union troops to cross the Potomac River and engage the Confederate forces in battle. There was a bridge but it was so narrow that the troops could cross only two abreast. The Confederates found this a great target and the Union troops were slaughtered. General Burnside didn't know that the river was only three feet deep and could have been forded safely at any point. President Lincoln later said of Burnside, "Only he could have wrung so spectacular a defeat from the jaws of victory."

- On January 22, 1879, British General Lord Chelmsford engaged the Zulus in warfare. The British were so confident of their ability to win that they decided it wasn't even worth their time to open in advance the iron-bound wooden ammunition boxes. They didn't realize until too late that someone forgot to bring along the crowbars needed to open the boxes. When their ammo ran out, the British were slaughtered by the Zulus. Many were found slumped over the boxes with their fingernails torn off in their efforts to claw the boxes open.

- In 1917 the British Admiralty decided to build a fleet of K-boats: 325-foot long, steam powered submarines. The K-boats were not successful. K2 caught fire on its maiden dive. K3 sank for no apparent reason (with the Prince of Wales aboard) and then mysteriously surfaced again. Later it was rammed by K6 and sank for good. K4 ran aground. K5 sank and all on board were killed. K6 got stuck on the bottom. K7 rammed K17 and went to the junk heap. K14 started leaking before ever leaving the dock, and was later rammed by K22 and sank. K17 went out of control and sank. K22 was rammed by an escorting cruiser. In 1918 the K project was abandoned after the deaths of some 250 British sailors.

War On The High Cheese

In the mid-1800s naval vessels of Brazil and Uruguay were engaged in battle when the Uruguayan ship ran out of shot for their cannons. The captain ordered his men to load the cannons with Dutch cheeses which were too old and hard to eat. The first two cheese cannonballs missed their mark, but the third one crashed into the mainmast of Brazil's ship. Two sailors nearby were killed by cheese shrapnel. After several more cheeses ripped their sails, the Brazilian ship fled.

War Is Hell, But Defense Is Peace

- President Harry Truman insisted that the Department of War be renamed the Department of Defense because it's easier for congressmen to get away with spending billions on defense than on war. In this line of thinking, perhaps we should refer to "World Defense I" and "World Defense II," call Tolstoy's novel *Defense and Peace* and change Sherman's comment to "Defense is Hell."
- Secretary of State Alexander Haig explained to the Senate Foreign Relations Committee in 1982 that weapons buildup by the U.S. was "absolutely essential to our hopes for meaningful arms reduction."
- When Lockheed was asked to design a cargo plane for the air force in 1951, the specifications totaled eight pages. In 1980 it took 2,750 pages. In 1943 Lockheed designed and built the first jet plane in just 143 days. The F/A-18 Hornet took nine years.
- In Pentagonese, a "pre-emptive counterattack" means we struck first; a "backloading of augmentation personnel" means a retreat; and a "predawn vertical insertion" is an invasion.
- After a bombing raid in Cambodia, Colonel David Opger told reporters, "You always write it's bombing, bombing, bombing. It's *not* bombing! It's air support!"

A New Weapon

Henry was born in 1761 in Britain. At the age of 18, he joined the army and by the age of 22, he had achieved the rank of second lieutenant. At this time he started working independently on a new weapon. He devoted all his spare time and much of his money to the project. Twenty years later, his new anti-personnel weapon was adopted by the British and Henry was subsequently promoted to lieutenant colonel. The weapon was named after its inventor— Henry Shrapnel. The first shrapnel was a shell filled with musket balls and a powder charge that was set off in mid-air, scattering the shot over a large area. Now the term "shrapnel" means any loose fragment from an explosive. Henry Shrapnel was eventually promoted to lieutenant general and died in 1802 at age 41. He was never paid for his invention.

The Final Fact

The military specifications for fruit cake are 18 pages long.

PRESIDENTS

The First Fact

The White House has 132 rooms, including a barbershop, theater, pool, doctor's office, dentist's office, bomb shelter, and 27 bathrooms.

In Chronological Order

- America had a vice-president before it had a president. John Adams was sworn in as VP several days before George Washington was sworn in as president.
- Washington's second inaugural address was the shortest on record at just 135 words. William Henry Harrison's inaugural address was the longest at 8,443 words.
- George Washington was sitting at dinner one evening when the heat from the fireplace behind him became so intense he had to move away from the hearth. A fellow diner joked that a general should be able to stand fire. Washington replied, "But it doesn't look good if he receives it from behind."
- John Adams lived longer than any other president. He was nearly 91 when he died.
- Jefferson has more descendents than any other president. Millard Fillmore has no descendents. Neither his son nor his daughter ever married.
- Jefferson was an accomplished violinist. He kept a pet mockingbird in the White House, which he taught to take food from his lips. He was among the first people in the U.S. to be inoculated against smallpox. He imported plants and was the first president to grow a tomato, which others still considered a dangerous plant. He loved to cook and introduced ice cream, waffles, and macaroni to the U.S.
- A visitor to Thomas Jefferson's office was outraged to find a newspaper there containing an editorial filled with contemptuous lies about the President. "Why don't you suppress this paper? Why don't you fine the editor, or throw him in jail?" asked the visitor. Jefferson answered, "Put that paper in your pocket, and if you hear the reality of our liberty, the freedom of the press, questioned—show them this paper and tell them where you found it."
- John Quincy Adams loved playing billiards and bought a billiard table for the White House. The public objected to the expense and he had to pay for it out of his own pocket.
- In his search for a cabinet he could work with, Andrew Jackson went through four Secretaries of State, five Secretaries of the Treasury, three Secretaries of War, three Secretaries of the Navy, three Attorney Generals, and two Postmaster Generals.
- Jackson was the first president to ever face an assassination attempt. A deranged man fired at him with two pistols, but both malfunctioned. Jackson then went after the man with his walking stick.
- Before he became president, Andrew Jackson fought a duel with Thomas Hart Benton. They both survived, but Jackson was left with a bullet lodged in his

left arm. Many years later, the bullet was removed by a surgeon. By now Jackson and Benton were good friends again, so Jackson offered to return the bullet to Benton, saying it was his property. Benton replied that since Jefferson had kept possession of the bullet for some 20 years, he could now be considered to be the owner. Jefferson pointed out that it had actually only been nineteen years since the duel, but Benton said, "In consideration of the extra care he has taken of it— kept it about his person and so on— I'll waive the odd year."

- John Tyler had more children than any other president, with 15. Eight were by his first wife, and seven by his second wife. Tyler's children by his first wife did not approve of his remarriage after their mother died and refused to attend the wedding.
- James Polk's family name was originally Pollock.
- At the time of his nomination, Zachary Taylor had never voted.
- James Buchanan was the only president who never married. At one point he was engaged, but after a fight his fiancé committed suicide.
- Abraham Lincoln was sick with smallpox when he gave the Gettysburg address.
- President Lincoln's young son, Tad, was made an honorary lieutenant by the Secretary of War. Tad took his job very seriously, wearing a miniature uniform and ordering various people about. He once sentenced a doll to death for falling asleep at its post. President Lincoln wrote out a pardon for the doll.
- When James Garfield was informed that Lincoln was dead, crowds in the streets clamored outside his window begging for a speech. Garfield stepped outside and said merely, "My fellow citizens, the President is dead, but the Government lives and God Omnipotent reigns."
- James Garfield could write Greek with one hand while writing Latin with the other.
- When Ulysses S. Grant was inaugurated in 1873, the temperature in Washington was 4°F. — the coldest inauguration day ever.
- Grant's daughter, Nellie, was born on the 4th of July and grew up thinking that the fireworks were in her honor. His son, Jesse, wanted to add to his stamp collection by using his father's influence to get American ambassadors abroad to send him foreign stamps. When his mother informed him that he'd have to write thank-you notes for the stamps, he decided not to be a stamp collector after all.
- President Chester Arthur never allowed his kids to be interviewed or photographed.
- Abe Lincoln's son Robert became President Arthur's Secretary of War.
- Within a span of three and a half years, Grover Cleveland was mayor of Buffalo; governor of New York state; and president of the U.S.
- When Cleveland's law partner had a baby girl, Cleveland gave him a gift of a baby carriage. That baby grew up to become Cleveland's bride.
- John Scott Harrison was a farmer born in Indiana, but he has the distinction of being the son of a president and the father of a president. His father was

President William Henry Harrison and his son was President Benjamin Harrison.
- On election night, Benjamin Harrison stayed up only until 11:00 p.m., then retired to bed before the election results were in. When a friend came by to congratulate him at midnight, he found the new president sound asleep. The next day he asked why he had retired so early. Harrison replied, "I knew that my staying up would not alter the result if I were defeated, while if I was elected I had a hard day in front of me. So a night's rest seemed the best in either event."
- When Benjamin Harrison arrived at the White House in 1889 with ten family members in tow, there was only one bathroom in the mansion. A professional rat-catcher had to be hired to take care of the rodent problem. When electricity was installed, the Harrison family slept with the lights on because everyone was afraid they'd be electrocuted if they touched the switches.
- During a tour, Benjamin Harrison made 140 speeches in 30 days and never repeated a single speech.
- William McKinley smoked cigars but refused to be photographed with one because he didn't want to set a bad example for kids.
- Theodore Roosevelt was vice-president when the hotel he was staying in caught fire and everyone was evacuated. Roosevelt shortly insisted on returning to his room, stating to a hotel official, "But I'm the vice-president!" The official let Roosevelt pass, then called to him, "What exactly are you vice-president of?" "The United States!" bellowed Roosevelt from the stairs. "Well, then— get back down here. I thought you were the vice-president of the hotel!"
- Theodore Roosevelt established the first press room in the White House after taking pity on some reporters who were shivering outside in the cold one day.
- When someone asked Teddy

On his first day in the White House, Calvin Coolidge pushed every button on his desk at once just to see all the people come running.

Roosevelt why he couldn't make his daughter Alice behave, he replied that he could either run the country or control Alice, but not both.
- In 1907 Theodore Roosevelt shook hands with 8,513 people, setting a record.

When Teddy Roosevelt's daughter Alice got married in the White House, the knife she was given to cut the cake was too small. She borrowed the sword of a nearby presidential aide and slashed the cake with that.

- One day Teddy had a friendly boxing match with a young naval officer. A blow to the left eye ruptured a blood vessel in Teddy's eye. His doctor warned him to cut out all strenuous activities until it healed if he wanted to save his eye. Teddy refused and gradually lost the sight in that eye. It was kept secret because he didn't want to hurt the feelings of the officer who had socked him in the eye.
- William Howard Taft's son, Charlie, brought along a copy of *Treasure Island* to read during his father's inaugural address.
- Woodrow Wilson had a typewriter that could be altered to print in either English or Greek.
- Wilson thought inaugural balls were frivolous and didn't have one.
- Edith Wilson, Woodrow's second wife, learned to ride a bike down the White House hallways.
- When he was governor of New Jersey, Woodrow Wilson received the news that a good friend of his who was a senator from New Jersey had just died. While he was still getting over the shock of the news, a prominent New Jersey politician called. "Governor," he said, "I would like to take the Senator's place." Wilson replied, "It's all right with me if it's all right with the undertaker!"
- Calvin Coolidge used to sit out on the White House porch in his rocking chair after dinner until crowds got so thick he had to give it up.
- Coolidge was born on the 4th of July.
- Coolidge had just been inaugurated and was staying at a hotel in Washington. He awoke to see a cat burglar going through his things. He watched the thief take his wallet, then a watch chain and charm. At this point Coolidge spoke up, saying, "I wouldn't take that if I were you— read what's on the back." The inscription was "Presented to Calvin Coolidge, Speaker of the House, by the Massachusetts General Court." Coolidge identified himself as the President of the United States. The burglar had no idea whose room he had broken into. Coolidge than led a quiet conversation with the man, finding out that he had

—Presidents— 125

broken into the room because he was a college student who did not have enough money to pay his hotel bill and get a train ticket back to campus. Coolidge counted out $32, saying it was a loan. The burglar left hastily, but later repaid the loan in full.

- A lady burst into Coolidge's office, exuberantly exclaiming over a wonderful speech he had just given. "The hall was so crowded," she exclaimed, "that I had to stand up all the way through your speech!" Coolidge replied, "So did I."
- After Coolidge announced that he "did not choose to run" for another term, a reporter asked him why not. "Because there's no chance for advancement," he replied.
- After leaving the presidency, Coolidge was filling out a form for the National Press Club. After name and address, the next space was marked "Occupation." He wrote "retired." The next spot said "comments." He wrote "Glad of it."

- Coolidge sent his dog to marine training school to learn some discipline. The dog flunked. When his cat, Tiger, turned up missing, Coolidge asked all the radio stations to broadcast a missing cat report. The cat was found, but later ran away again and never returned.
- Herbert Hoover never accepted his presidential salary.
- Hoover once received a request from an autograph collector asking for three of Hoover's signatures. He explained that he wanted one for himself and two to trade for a Babe Ruth signature since "it takes two of yours to get one of Babe Ruth's." Hoover was amused and sent the three signatures.
- Franklin D. Roosevelt was paralyzed from the waist down as the result of a bout with polio he suffered in 1921. During his entire 12-year presidency, he could not walk a step without braces and crutches. Yet he traveled more than any previous president, wrestled with his sons, and swam.
- Harry S. Truman had no middle name beyond the letter S.
- Truman was the only 20th-century president who never attended college. By the age of 14 he had read every book in the Independence, Missouri library.
- Truman met his future wife, Bess, when he was just six years old. She was the only girl in town who could whistle through her teeth.
- Truman had to order special cars built to accommodate the tall top hats which he occasionally wore.
- Lincoln was the tallest president at six feet four inches, but Lyndon B. Johnson was the second tallest at just one inch shorter.
- When Bill Moyers was Johnson's press secretary, he was asked to dinner one night. Johnson requested that Moyers say grace, but complained halfway through the prayer, telling Moyers to pray louder because he couldn't hear.

Moyers replied, "I wasn't talking to you, Mr. President."
- Nixon's beard grew so fast he often had to shave two or three times a day.
- When President Carter hosted the two-hour show "Ask Mr. Carter," nine million people called in with questions or advice for the President, but only 42 of the calls actually got through and appeared on the show.
- President Carter was asked how he would feel if he found out his daughter was having an affair. "Shocked and overwhelmed," he exclaimed. "But then, she's only seven years old!"
- During a televised speech concerning the budget, President Reagan used a handful of small change to illustrate the value of a dollar. "It takes a real actor to do that," said an analyst. "Carter would have emphasized all the wrong words. Ford would have fumbled and dropped the cash. Nixon would have pocketed it."

The Final Fact

A pastry chef once baked 18,000 cookies for a single reception for Jimmy Carter.

MEDICAL BREAKTHROUGHS

The First Fact

Until the middle of the 1800s, only half the children born in the U.S. reached their fifth birthday. Since 1850 all ten leading causes of infant death have been cured. Today only 25 out of 1,000 babies die. Between 1800 and 1900 more major medical advances were made than had occurred in the entire previous history of mankind.

Inception Of Incubators

Dr. Martin Couney was a young doctor at a French maternity hospital in 1896 when the hospital developed the first incubators for premature infants. The incubators were so successful that Dr. Couney was asked to demonstrate them at an international exposition in Berlin. The exhibit, complete with premature babies supplied by German hospitals, was a smash hit. Couney brought his incubator show to America and set it up on Coney Island. It attracted such crowds that he built an ornate "Baby Palace" and hired barkers to bring the crowds in. Taking the show on the road, he and his premature babies traveled the country, earning stupendous amounts of money. However, it took the medical profession decades to catch on to the value of the infant incubator. When incubators finally became standard equipment in maternity wards, Couney's popularity as a side show fell off. Couney claimed that of the 8,000 preemies he had exhibited, 6,500 survived. One of his barkers, an unknown Englishman named Archibald Leach, went on to become a famous Hollywood actor: Cary Grant.

Wounds And Wonders

- In the 1500s Amboise Paré was a French surgeon who specialized in battlefield injuries. It was the custom of the day to pour boiling oil on wounds to stop the bleeding. After one battle, Paré ran out of hot oil. He bandaged the wounds of the remaining men as best he could with herbs and salves. In the weeks that followed, he was amazed to find that those men who had not received the standard hot oil treatment were recovering much more quickly. Later Paré became the first man to discover that during amputation, tourniquets and tying the arteries worked much better than using the red hot irons that were the method of the day.
- Joseph Lister, a surgeon in the late 1800s, was perplexed: Why, when a person broke a bone, would the bone heal well if it was a simple fracture (with the skin remaining intact), but when the skin was broken in a compound fracture, infection and death were almost certain to follow? Then Lister read a paper written by Louis Pasteur which said infection can be caused by airborne germs. Lister began a thorough and productive study of what killed germs. He championed the idea that wounds should be kept sterile using an *antiseptic*, from the Greek words for 'against decay.' Today he is memorialized in Listerine mouthwash.

- During the Civil War, there were hundreds of Union and Confederate wounded at the Union camp in Chattanooga. Unfortunately, there were few medical supplies. Because it was a Union camp, the Union soldiers received the bulk of the medicine. The Confederate wounded were given nothing. Their wounds inevitably became infested with maggots. Ironically, the Confederates healed more quickly. The doctors had stumbled upon a medical fact: maggots help stop the growth of bacteria and keep open wounds clean.

Early Inventions

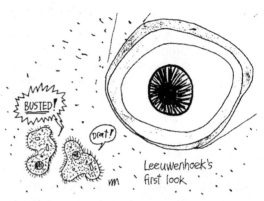

Leeuwenhoek's first look

- Dutch scientist Anthony Van Leeuwenhoek was the first person to see germs when he invented the microscope in the middle 1600s. He sent accounts of what he found to interested British scientists. However, he jealously guarded the secret of building microscopes and refused to send any of the instruments to other researchers. As a result, the secret of the microscope died with him. It was years before his experiments could be re-created. Leeuwenhoek never discovered that the germs he was observing were the cause of disease.
- Leopold Auenbrugger was a doctor in Vienna in the 1700s. His father had been an innkeeper who often drew wine from large casks in the cellar. Leopold watched his dad pound on the casks to find out how much wine each contained— if he tapped above the wine level, the sound was hollow. Below the wine level, the sound was flat. When Leopold became a doctor, he saw many cases of tuberculosis in which the lungs fill with fluid. Remembering the casks, he began to pound on patient's chests and backs. He was able to tell if there was fluid in the lungs just by listening. He published a paper on his findings, but the idea did not catch on for another 50 years. Today every doctor pounds on the chest during a physical exam.
- One person who read about Leopold's discovery was a French doctor named Laennec. He made it a habit of pounding on people's chests, but in 1819 a woman came to see him who was so fat that he couldn't hear much. Then one day he saw children playing on a pile of lumber. One child would tap or scratch on the end of a long beam while the others listened at the other end. The sound carried, amusing the kids. This inspired an idea. The next time Laennec saw his fat patient, he rolled a sheet of paper into a cylinder, placed one end on her chest and the other end to his ear. He was able to clearly hear her heartbeat and breathing. The resulting invention is called the *stethoscope,* from the Greek words meaning 'the chest' and 'to observe.'

- In 1895 a man named Roentgen stumbled upon some invisible light rays that could pass through certain substances but not through others. He named them X-rays because X stands for an unknown integer.

Smallpox Defeated

In George Washington's day, one out of every five people in London bore the scars of smallpox. George Washington did, although he's usually portrayed with clear skin. One out of every three children died of smallpox before their third birthday. In the 1700s European people realized that if you recovered from smallpox, you would never get the disease again. Whenever a person came down with a mild, survivable form of smallpox, it was fashionable to organize smallpox parties. Friends and relatives would gather in one house in order to catch the mild form of the disease together, and thus become immune to more deadly strains. In that day, milkmaids were well-known for their clear, unpocked skin. It was common for milkmaids to catch cowpox from the animals they were milking, and an old wive's tale said that people who had cowpox would never catch smallpox. In 1796 Edward Jenner, an English doctor, was the first person to confirm this belief as the truth. He inoculated an eight-year-old boy with cowpox. Six weeks later, he inoculated the boy with smallpox. The boy did not get smallpox. At first this discovery was ridiculed in the medical society, but when Napoleon, Thomas Jefferson, and Benjamin Franklin endorsed the idea, Jenner became rich and famous. He had invented vaccination. The word comes from *vaccinia*, the Latin word for cow.

Fact

In 1350 the Bubonic Plague swept through Europe, killing a quarter of the population. To guard against the plague, Venice required all foreign ships entering the harbor to wait 40 days before they were allowed to land. The Italian word for forty is *quarant*, leading to our word quarantine.

Another Fact

When Captain Cook landed on Hawaii in 1778, he found 300,000 healthy natives there. However, he and subsequent explorers brought germs the natives had never been exposed to. By 1860 there were fewer than 37,000 Hawaiians. When Cortez arrived in Mexico in 1520, he brought smallpox with him and about half the native population died, contributing to their defeat. In the American west, smallpox-infested blankets were deliberately given to unsuspecting Indians.

Mysterious Mosquito Maladies

- Until this century, half of all human deaths could be traced to mosquitoes. The malaria protozoa carried by mosquitoes are estimated to be the most widespread parasites in the world. Malaria has caused more deaths than all wars put together. During the Spanish-American war, more soldiers died from malaria and yellow fever than were killed in combat. During the digging of the Panama Canal, malaria and yellow fever caused so many deaths that the project had to be halted. A Havana doctor was the first to guess that the mosquito was the carrier of the two diseases. He was thought to be a crackpot, but several other doctors were so desperate to find a cure that they decided to test the theory. Two physicians, James Carroll and Jesse Lazear, let mosquitoes feed on patients ill with yellow fever. Then they took a desperate but necessary chance— they let the mosquitoes feed on their own arms. Both men came down with yellow fever. The theory was proven. Carroll recovered, but Lazear died. An anti-mosquito campaign was launched, and a few years later the Panama Canal was completed.

- The word malaria means "bad air" which was thought to be the source of the disease. South American Indians used cinchona bark to combat malaria for hundreds of years. One member of a Spanish exploratory party was left for dead when he came down with malaria. Thirsty, he crawled to a pool of water that had collected on the ground and drank. He made a remarkable recovery, and when his party passed by again they were amazed to find him well. He showed them the pool he had drunk from— there was a piece of cinchona floating in it. Cinchona bark is still used to treat malarial symptoms today. It's called quinine.

The Magic Bullet

Alexander Fleming was a member of England's medical corps during World War I. He was studying bacteria by growing them on culture plates. One day he noticed one of his culture plates had been contaminated by mold. He was about to toss out the whole thing when he noticed that the bacteria had all died in a circle around the mold. The mold was a member of the *penicillium* family, commonly found on old bread and rotting fruit. It also gives Roquefort cheese its blue veins. Intrigued, he grew more of the mold until he had enough to begin extracting some of the fluids that killed microbes. Even when greatly diluted, the liquid would kill many kinds of germs without harming the body. In 1929 he wrote a paper about his research, but because the mold was too difficult to grow in large amounts, the discovery went unnoticed. A decade later, Dr. Howard Florey in Oxford, England, read Flemming's paper and wrote to the doctor asking for some samples of the mold. He set up row upon row of mold-growing flasks until he had extracted enough fluid from them to treat one case of infection. A young policeman was dying of blood poisoning, so Dr. Florey began to give him daily doses of the new drug, penicillin. His improvement was dramatic— but then the small supply of penicillin ran out. The man suffered a recurrence of the sickness and died. Still, it was obvious to all that penicillin had been the cure, if only larger amounts had been available. Dr. Florey tried to get the British government to help him grow the mold on a large scale, but they were so busy with World War II that they could not help. But the U.S. Government, desperate to save the wounded soldiers dying of infection, began growing it in huge tanks. By 1944 there was enough penicillin even civilians could benefit from it.

Fact

The word penicillin comes from the Latin word for brush because an artist's brush had wispy hairs just like the mold does. That's also where we get the word pencil, because people used to write with brushes. The ancient Egyptians sometimes placed moldy bread over wounds.

A Tragic Tale

There is a valley high in the Andes between Peru and Chili that not even the bravest natives dared pass through at night. Mysteriously, all those who traveled the pass in the daylight arrived safely on the other side, but those who went at night invariably died of a fatal anemia. Only a few rare people survived the unexplainable illness, and they were forever afterwards immune. Finally a Peruvian medical student named Carrion identified a sandfly so small that it can easily slip through mosquito netting. The fly carries the germ that causes the deadly anemia. Since the sandfly avoids light, it comes out only at night, biting any handy animal and injecting the disease. In order to positively prove his theory, Carrion injected himself with a serum made from the sandflies, and proved himself correct with his own death. The disease now carries his name.

Another Tragic Tale

In the 1800s people knew that disease was more common in dirty places than clean ones, but they didn't know why. It was common for physicians to go from one sick patient to the next without bothering to wash their hands, clean their instruments, or change their blood-stained clothing. In 1846 a Hungarian doctor named Semmelweis was working in the obstetrics unit of an Austrian hospital. He noticed that up to 30% of new mothers attended by physicians died of blood poisoning after giving birth. Yet in another obstetrics unit in the same hospital where the women were tended by midwives, very few new mothers died. The difference between the two units, he discovered, was that the midwives frequently washed their hands, whereas the doctors never did. Even after dissecting dead bodies, doctors would not wash their hands before examining women in childbirth. They felt that bloody clothing and dirty hands were the sign of a busy physician. Semmelweis ordered people working in his ward to wash their hands between every patient, and soon the death rate was down to 1%. But the doctors ridiculed him, insisting that the deaths were caused by bad air, poor diet, or depression— not unwashed hands. In their ward, the death rate remained high. Strained by the nervous tension and upset at the needless deaths of so many young women, Semmelweis went insane. He died in an asylum at the age of 47 of blood poisoning— the very disease he had been trying to eradicate.

American Epidemics

- 67% of illnesses treated today are preventable.
- We spend $425 billion annually on medical care. It's estimated that one quarter of that goes for preventable problems, and another quarter goes for unnecessary surgeries.
- One out of five men and one out of four women are at least 10% overweight.
- One out of every four people will get cancer during their lifetime.
- Between the ages of 65 and 70, the death rate among retired men is higher than for those who continue to work.

The Final Fact

A black child born within five miles of Washington D.C. today has less of a chance of living a single year than a similar child born in Jamaica, Tobago, or Trinidad.

QUICK BITS

The First Fact

The average lifespan of an umbrella is one and a half years.

Misc. Bits

- In 1811 the U.S. Treasury Department set up a 'conscience fund.' Whenever anyone sends money to the government because they feel guilty for cheating on their taxes or stealing government property, the money is put into the fund. About a quarter of a million dollars per year is sent in.
- The first person to receive a Social Security check was Ida Fuller of Vermont who received check #00-000-001 for $22 on Jan. 31, 1940.
- Actor Conrad Cantzen left $227,000 in his will to provide shoes for unemployed actors.
- Daisy Alexander inherited the Singer sewing machine fortune. She didn't know what to do with her money when she died, so she sealed her will in a bottle and tossed it in the River Thames in London. The will gave 50% of her fortune to whomever found the bottle. She died two years later. Ten years later an unemployed restaurant worker named Jack Wurm found the bottle on the beach at San Francisco. He received some $6 million. Daisy's lawyer got the other half.
- A 15th century satirist named Rabelais said in his will, "I have nothing, I owe a great deal; the rest I give to the poor."
- If you had invested $5,000 in Avon in 1950, the investment would be worth over $2 million today.
- The average recording star earns four cents for every single and 25 cents for each album sold.
- Americans spend 20% of their food budget eating out.

Quick Bits About Holidays

- 36% of all bills passed by Congress since 1985 have dealt with establishing commemorative days, weeks, or months.
- 50% of all mail sent in 1985 consisted of greeting cards.
- There are more phone calls placed on Mother's Day than on any other day of the year.
- More Americans eat out on Mother's Day than on any other day.
- Only 25% of Christmases in New York City are white, but 75% are white in Minneapolis.
- Some 60 wreaths are sent to Graceland on Elvis's birthday each year.

Beard Bits

- Alexander the Great ordered all of his soldiers to shave their beards before a battle to prevent the enemy from grabbing hold of them.
- British statesman Augustus Keppel was in his early 20s when he was sent as a messenger to the leader of Algiers. The Algerian commander laughed at the

youth, saying the King of England must not be very bright to send a beardless youth as a negotiator. Keppel replied, "Had my master supposed that wisdom was measured by the length of the beard, he would have sent you a billy goat."
- Actor John Drew always wore a mustache, until he had to shave it off to play a part. Soon after, he met an acquaintance of his, Max Beerbohm, but failed to recognize him. Beerbohm recognized Drew and said, "Mr. Drew, I'm afraid you don't recognize me without your mustache."
- Artist Salvador Dali had a fabulous mustache that he waxed. The mustache curled up to his eyes. While staying in a New York hotel, he walked up and down the corridors ringing a small silver bell. A friend asked him why he was ringing the bell. "I carry it and I ring it so people will see my mustaches," he explained.
- Czar Peter I of Russia ordered all men to shave their beards. Those who did not had to pay a beard tax. Some people surmise that the reason for this law was that the Czar was unable to grow a beard himself.

More Misc. Bits

- Zoologist Desmond Morris gave a bunch of apes in a zoo art supplies and was interested to see that they created thoughtful and interesting pictures. But when he started giving them peanuts as payment for their drawings, the quality of their work deteriorated and they turned in hastily scrawled scribbles just to get the reward.
- There are 68,000 convenience stores in the U.S.
- Only 5% of defense contracts are awarded through competitive bidding.
- There are 3,650 astronomers in the U.S., and 15,000 astrologers.
- 48% of astronauts say they have experienced motion sickness in space.
- When Ronald Reagan's daughter Patti got married, there were 134 guests and 180 Secret Service agents in attendance.
- Half of first-time brides in Kentucky are teenagers.
- 16% of men earning less than $5,000 annually say they cheat on their wives, and 70% of those earning over $70,000 say they do.
- The average American marriage lasts 9.4 years.

Fast Facts About American Health

- The average person spends 10% of their income on health care.
- 15% of people under the age of 65 have no health insurance.
- 41% of the money spent on health care is paid for by the government.
- 28% of Medicare funds go to people with less than a year to live.
- There are about 300 Americans who have someone else's heart.
- About 225 sex change operations are performed in the U.S. each year.
- There are 13 people cryogenically frozen in hopes of being brought back to life.

- 24% of women receive no prenatal care during the first three months of pregnancy.
- In 1973, 27% of fathers were in the delivery room when their children were born. Today, 79% are.

Still More Misc. Bits About America

- The average home buyer looks at 14 homes before making a purchase.
- The average American lives in 30 different houses in a lifetime.
- 4.6% live in mobile homes.
- 6% say they find life dull.
- 48% report that they regularly sing, hum, or whistle.
- 20% of men say they would wear a pair of uncomfortable shoes because they look good. 45% of women say they would.
- 40% of parents say they never read to their children. 27% say they never help them with their homework.
- 45% of adults polled said they have never read a book.
- 11% of people in a survey responded that they believe America has never used a nuclear weapon in a war.
- 27 of the 50 states have nuclear weapons deployed in them.
- 10% of Californians have earthquake insurance.
- The average 15-year-old has eight cavities.
- 25% of all products sold in America today are imported.
- 70% of Japanese over the age of 60 live with younger relatives. Only 6.3% of Americans do.
- There are about 10,000 draft resisters still living in Canada.
- There are more streets named Park in America than any other street name. Main ranks #32.
- The average electric bill for a night game at Shea Stadium is $12,000.
- In 1984 less than 2% of Japan's research and development funds were provided by the government. In that same year, almost 33% of America's R & D funds came from the government.

It's estimated that 10% of resumés contain a fabricated job or college degree, and that half a million Americans have phony diplomas.

Fast Facts

- An average 40-minute Henny Youngman comedy routine contains 245 jokes.
- Only .01% of all life forms known to have existed in the history of the planet still exist today.
- In 1985 half of Bolivia's export earnings came from cocaine.
- In 1985 England hosted the International Conference on Spelling Reform. 17 people attended.
- 50% of defectors eventually return to their homeland.

There are 400 coffin manufacturers in the U.S.

Strange But True

In 1848 Niagara Falls stopped running. Early in the morning on March 29, people nearby awakened to the sound of silence. Rushing out to look at the falls, they saw that there was no water going over Niagara. Only a few pools and ponds remained in the gorge below, and a few tiny trickles running down from the lip of the falls. As day broke, many went down to walk on the dry river bottom. They were astonished at the smoothness of the boulders at the bottom. Some found artifacts from unfortunate people who had gone over the falls. Many knelt to pray, expecting the end of the world at any moment. Huge crowds waited on the edge of the falls for the return of the river. Thirty hours later, a great roar heralded the return of the water. Many scavengers barely made it out of the way in time. The Niagara was back. What caused the stoppage? High winds and heavy ice floes had dammed the outlet of Lake Erie, completely shutting off the flow of water to the river. A sudden shift in the wind broke the ice jam and released the water.

Crime Statistics

- Only 1% of missing children are abducted by strangers.
- Less than 1% of cops in New York City fired their guns in the line of duty in 1985.
- 50% of people believe those accused of a crime are guilty by law until proven innocent.

- Over 16,000 people have received new identities under the Federal Witness Security Program.
- 85% of all hostage deaths in airplane hijackings since 1968 have occurred during rescue attempts.
- 39% of death row inmates either commit suicide, are murdered, or die of natural causes before their execution can take place.
- Each week in the U.S., the population of state and federal prisons increases by 1,000.
- In Canton, China, you can hire a bodyguard for $3 a day. In New York City it'll cost you $250 per day.
- Only 9% of burglaries in the U.S. are ever solved.
- There has only been one armed robbery in the entire history of Iceland.
- In New York City in 1985, 1,800 people were issued summons for jaywalking. In the same year, 50,000 people were cited in L.A.

Quote

John Hylan, mayor of New York City in 1922, denied that there was a crime problem in his town, saying, "The police are fully able to meet and compete with the criminals!"

Television Bits

- The average American sees 69 Coca-Cola commercials annually.
- The TV show *Dallas* is shown in 98 different nations worldwide.
- 62% of children's TV shows are based on toys.
- 51% of TV sets have a remote control.

Poverty Facts

- 24% of divorced mothers do not receive the child support they are entitled to.
- L.A. ranks first in the number of homeless people living on the streets.
- 40% of children in New York City live in poverty.
- 47% of black children nationwide live in poverty.
- 65% of Brazilians suffer from malnutrition.

Job Facts

- 45% of Americans over the age of 50 say their current occupation is different from what they planned on doing when they were young.
- One out of every 25 residents of Washington D.C. is a lawyer.
- The average American business lunch lasts 67 minutes, but the average French business lunch lasts 124 minutes.
- There's been a 26% decrease in the buying power of minimum wage since 1981.
- 60,000 people quit their jobs each workday. 12,000 are fired.

- 75% of unemployed Americans receive no unemployment benefits.
- The average worker has held eight jobs by the age of 40.

Solution To Poverty

French novelist Honoré Balzac lived in poverty before becoming successful. In his unfurnished room, Balzac penciled the words "rosewood paneling" on one bare wall; "tapestry with Venetian mirror" on another; and "picture by Raphael" over the fireplace.

Some More Misc. Bits

- 90% of refrigerators are either white or almond.
- 33% of Americans have never flown in an airplane.
- 39% of Americans say they never go to movies.
- There have been over 2,000 referendums on water fluoridation in the U.S. since 1950, and 60% of them have been voted down.
- In 1955, 10% of households contained just one person. Today, 25% do.
- 66% of Americans don't know how long a meter is.
- There are 376 one-room schoolhouses in Nebraska.
- China's top female fashion model earns $70 per month.
- 47% of the population of Nicaragua is under the age of 15.
- In 1985 the University of Alabama spent $8.6 million on its athletic department, and $1.1 million on its physics department.
- The average person learns and remembers 10,000 different faces throughout their lifetime.
- Pepsi had to sell 192,307,692 cans of pop to recoup the cost of its Michael Jackson ad campaign.

A Real Genius

Willis Dysart was a mathematical genius, able to figure colossal numbers in his head faster than anyone could do it on a calculator. He could multiply seven digit numbers in five seconds or less. In 1949 when he was 16, he was invited by a Minnesota newspaper to help figure election results. He stood in front of a radio microphone, tabulating the results as quickly as they came in. At any given moment he was able to give the current standing of any candidate as well as the percentage of votes tallied and the probable outcome based on current results. He told how many years, months, days, hours, and seconds each candidate had lived. The newspaper that hired him scored some memorable scoops, printed while other papers were still tallying results. Once a building contractor went to Willis saying he had to build a large schoolhouse. He told Willis the dimensions of the building and the size of the bricks. He wanted to know how many bricks he would need. Willis told him. When the school was finished, the contractor had half a brick left over.

The Final Fact

If Barbie were life-size, her measurements would be 39-23-33.

VITAMINS

The First Fact
There are no Betty Rubble tablets in a bottle of Flintstone Chewable Vitamins.

The ABCs Of Vitamins
In the early 1900s chemists fed rats controlled diets in order to isolate vitamins essential for good health. The first vitamin they identified prevented eye disorders. Because they didn't know what to name it, they called it simply vitamin "A." Next they found that beriberi was cured with what they dubbed vitamin "B." Vitamin C prevented scurvy and vitamin D prevented rickets. At one time there were vitamins A through P. Subsequent research revealed many duplicates, so some were scratched from the list. That's why there is no vitamin F today. Later it was discovered that vitamin B was actually a complex compound, and it was broken down into vitamins B1 through B14. Again, later studies showed some errors. Today we have only B1, B2, B6, and B12. Today we know there are 13 vitamins: A, B1, B2, B6, B12, C, D, E, K, niacin, pantothenic acid, biotin, and folic acid. In 1933 scientists learned how to manufacture synthetic vitamins in the laboratory, paving the way for the vitamin industry.

Fact
In a test at the University of Texas, rats were fed one food only. Two-thirds of the rats fed white bread died after 90 days. Rats fared little better when fed only peanuts, hot dogs, hamburger, shredded wheat, or macaroni. They lived somewhat longer on tuna or milk. The best single food was egg.

Vitamin A
Elmer McCollum is the man who pioneered research in vitamin discovery. He nearly died of vitamin deficiency himself as a child. Born in 1879, he was very sickly. One day he was fussing on his mother's lap as she was peeling apples. She gave him some apple scrapings to quiet him, and he liked them. In the next few days she fed him as much apple as he wanted, and he made a remarkable recovery. He had been suffering from the first symptoms of scurvy, a disease caused by the lack of vitamin C. It was another 50 years before that vitamin was isolated.

After college, he got a job as a researcher at the University of Wisconsin. The college was trying to discover whether wheat, oats, or corn was the best feed for cows. Their methods were simply to give three different groups of cows the three different feeds and see what happened. The wheat-fed cows went blind. The oat-fed cows gave birth to dead calves. Only the corn-fed cows were healthy. Next McCollum switched his research methods to rats because their shorter lives made research easier. He fed his rats a mixture of protein, carbohydrates, minerals, and fat. He discovered that when the source of fat was butter or egg yolk, the rats remained healthy. But when he switched the fat to olive oil, the rats died.

Obviously there was something essential in butter and eggs that was not present in olive oil. After much research, the substance was identified, extracted, and named vitamin A.

Vitamin A Overdose Warning

In January of 1969 some Dutch fishermen off the coast of Norway caught a halibut that was over six feet long. Its liver was big enough to feed the whole crew. Eleven of the twelve men gorged on liver that night. One man hated liver and refused to eat any. Soon the men who had eaten the liver were sick. Their skin became red and swollen, and by the next morning, it was peeling off as if they'd been badly sunburned. Only the man who had eaten none of the liver was unaffected. The sailors were suffering from hypervitaminosis A— an overdose. They had ingested the equivalent of 2,000 multivitamin tablets. The livers of many fish and also polar bears hold concentrates of vitamin A. Taking too much of this vitamin can result in symptoms including loss of appetite, roughness of the skin, headaches, itching, loss of hair, vomiting, fatigue, swelling in the feet and arms, and even an increase in brain fluid.

The daily allotment of vitamin A is about .0001 ounce. Vitamins A, D, E, and K are fat soluble and collect in the body tissues rather than being flushed out. These are the vitamins that can be overdosed. Beef liver contains 60,000 IU of vitamin A in four ounces; polar bear liver, however, is about 10 times richer than that.

Vitamin B

Vitamin B12 is necessary for the formation of red corpuscles in the blood, for normal growth, and for maintenance of healthy nerve cells. You only need .00000014 of an ounce of vitamin B12 each day, but a lack of that tiny amount can be fatal. It is impossible to get B12 on a strict vegetarian diet. For a long time scientists wondered why Hindus, who are strict vegetarians, never suffered from deficiencies while living in India, but would come down with B12 deficiencies if they emigrated to Britain. It was found that their diet in India inadvertently contained insect parts that became mixed in with the food. But in Britain, where food control laws were stricter, there were fewer microscopic insect fragments in the food. Insects are rich in vitamins, including B12.

B Is For Beriberi

Beriberi was a widespread disease causing weakness and death. In the late 1800s a doctor named Eijkman was trying to isolate the beriberi germ at a hospital. Suddenly the chickens kept in the hospital yard came down with beriberi. The doctor began to study the birds, but they all unexpectedly recovered. The doctor questioned the chickens' keeper. The keeper told him that the birds had been eating chicken feed until the supply ran out. Then they were fed white rice from the hospital kitchen. While on a white rice diet, all became sick. When the hospital director discovered that the chickens were eating white rice, he ordered they be fed cheaper brown rice instead. The chickens recovered soon after. Intrigued, the doctor again fed the chickens only white rice. Soon they were ill. When he gave them brown rice, they recovered. He theorized that the illness was caused by poisons in the white rice— poisons that were neutralized in brown rice.

Brown rice is rice with the husk left on. Oils in the husk cause the grain to spoil faster than if it is polished off. Polished rice (white rice) keeps longer, but lacks the nutrition found in the husks. Vitamin B was the substance that cured beriberi. It was years before this became known.

Alcoholics are prone to beriberi because blood alcohol prevents the absorption of vitamin B. Symptoms include irritability, depression, fatigue, constipation, and loss of appetite. Beriberi is also relatively common in Japan, where primary dietary components include raw fish and polished rice. Raw fish contains an enzyme that destroys vitamin B.

Vitamin C

In earlier centuries, scurvy was a disease striking sailors, prisoners, armies, and besieged cities. Victims got progressively weaker and eventually died. In 1737 an Austrian doctor named Kramer noticed army soldiers often got scurvy, but officers (who ate better food) never did. He was the first person to make the connection between diet and disease. After Kramer's report came out, a Scottish doctor named Lind revealed Canadian Indians once saved a ship full of scurvy-ridden French explorers by giving them pine needle tea. His subsequent experiments proved citrus fruits would prevent scurvy. Captain Cook was so impressed he took limes on his round-the-world voyage, and lost only one sailor to the disease. However, the British army remained unconvinced and didn't start following the advice for another 40 years. In 1794 the British Admiralty finally decided to try citrus as a preventative for scurvy. They sent an English squadron out with a full supply of lemons. When the ships touched port at Madras 23 weeks later, only one crewman had come down with scurvy— and he had traded his daily lemon juice ration for another sailor's rum.

After it was discovered that citrus fruits could cure scurvy, every Spanish sailor bound for the Americas was supplied with 100 seeds or young seedlings to be planted in the new land. Today's Florida groves began with trees planted in 1513 by Ponce de Leon. By 1800 scurvy was wiped out. Because lemons were commonly called limes, English seaman eventually became known as "limeys."

Without vitamin C, the body cannot synthesize collagen, the adhesive protein substance holding cells together. Without collagen, wounds cannot heal, old scars open, and gums rot. The victim becomes cranky, apathetic, and dizzy; joints and muscles become sore; splotches appear around the roots of the hair; breath becomes foul; bones grow brittle; legs swell; and bruises appear as blood vessels rupture. Death occurs when the brain, lungs, or digestive tract rupture.

Fast Facts

- One potato a day is enough to ward off scurvy.
- Vitamin C, when taken with iron, will increase the absorption and utilization of iron.
- Bruising easily can be a sign of a mild vitamin C deficiency.
- Guavas, a tropical fruit, have six times as much vitamin C as oranges. Turnip greens, green peppers, raw broccoli, and parsley all exceed oranges in vitamin C content.
- People need to increase their intake of Vitamin C if they are pregnant, breast feeding, recovering from surgery, living in a cold environment, under stress, suffering from infections, burns, or diarrhea, or perspiring more than normal.

Vitamin D

Vitamin D acts as a catalyst to produce proteins allowing minerals to move through the intestinal membrane and into the cells. The misperception persists that vitamin D is present in sunlight. Actually, vitamin D cannot be formed *unless* it is activated by ultraviolet light. Therefore, sunlight does not contain vitamin D; it only activates it. Cats and dogs, when they lick their fur, ingest body fat that has been irradiated on their coats. This serves as a source of vitamin D. One school of thought holds that black skin evolved as protection against sunburn and skin cancer. Other scientists feel white skin evolved as a measure to allow enough ultraviolet light to pass through the skin in cold climates where people wear heavy clothing and their exposure to sunlight is limited.

Too much vitamin D can release the body's store of calcium and phosphorus from the bones, redepositing it along the walls of the blood vessels, in the heart, the kidneys, and the bronchial passages— and this can be fatal. It can also lead to calcium being deposited at the ends of long bones, interfering with normal bone growth.

Quick Bits

- There are 43 nutrients which are considered essential to health and growth. Mineral elements account for 17 of the 43, and they account for about 4% of body weight. Calcium and phosphorus make up three-quarters of that 4%.

- Carrots don't contain vitamin A; they contain carotene, which the liver *converts* to vitamin A.
- Unfortified milk has only tiny traces of vitamin D. Vitamin D is found in egg yolk and fish liver oil, but nowhere else.
- Due to improved diet, 25% of American men now reach heights of six feet or greater, compared to 4% in 1900.

N Is For Niacin

Pellagra is Italian for "rough skin." It's a disease that was very widespread until recently. The first symptom is irritated skin, and it is eventually fatal if left untreated. In the early 1900s the disease was rampant in the deep south. The Public Health Service hired Joseph Goldberger to track down the cause. Goldberger's first discovery was that pellagra was widespread among prison inmates, children in orphanages, and patients in mental institutions. Yet all of his research failed to produce a single doctor, nurse, nun, or prison guard who also had the disease. Theory held pellagra was a contagious disease, but Goldberger became convinced it was tied to the diet. In the Methodist Orphan Asylum in Jackson, Mississippi, one-third of the children suffered from pellagra. However, *all* of the victims were between the ages of six and twelve. He discovered only the children between the ages of one and five were given milk to drink. And only the children over the age of twelve were given much meat. Between the age of six and twelve, the orphans received no milk and little meat. They survived on grits, mush, and sow belly. And they got pellagra. Goldberger convinced the orphanage to change the children's diet, giving them lots of meat, milk, and eggs. Pellagra disappeared.

Wanting to be thorough, Goldberger decided if he could cure the disease with proper diet, he ought to be able to induce it through faulty diet. At the prison farm near Jackson, he signed up twelve prisoners who were willing to go on a special diet in exchange for a pardon at the end of six months. He fed them biscuits, mush, grits, gravy, syrup, corn bread, greens, sweet potatoes, rice, coffee and sugar. After a few weeks, the men got pellagra. Goldberger went one step further to prove the illness was not contagious. He collected 16 volunteers, including his wife and himself, who did everything possible to contract the pellagra infection through injections and secretions and bodily contact with sufferers. No one got the disease. Goldberger spent the rest of his life in the laboratory trying to discover what factor meat, milk, and egg yolks had in common. In 1937, eight years after his death, niacin was identified and isolated.

Identifying the vitamin that exists in air.

Vitamin E

Vitamin E is necessary for reproduction. Many people have concluded that massive doses of vitamin E should improve the love life. But vitamin E's role in reproduction is merely to prevent miscarriage and has nothing to do with sex or conception.

Vitamin K

Vitamin K comes in cabbage, cauliflower, spinach, and pork liver, but the vitamin is also synthesized in the intestinal tract by bacteria, no matter what you eat. Vitamin K is needed for the liver to synthesize clotting elements that circulate in the blood. Too much vitamin K can damage the liver. Taking oral antibiotics can kill the intestinal bacteria that synthesize vitamin K.

Popeye's Sorrow

In the early days of vitamin and mineral research, a chemist put a decimal point in the wrong place, mistakenly endowing spinach with ten times the amount of iron it actually contains. The myth that spinach is extraordinarily high in iron still survives. Spinach has iron, but many foods, including soy beans, peas, beets, sunflower seeds, and nuts have more. To get your annual requirement of iron from spinach alone, you'd have to eat twice your weight in spinach yearly. This wouldn't be a good idea because it contains a compound that increases the chances of kidney stones. Still, when Popeye started eating spinach, sales soared.

The Final Fact

11% of Americans consume five or more vitamin pills each day.

RULERS & ROYALTY

The First Fact

After King Farouk I of Egypt was driven from his throne in a 1952 coup, he remarked, "One day there will only be five kings left: hearts, spades, diamonds, clubs, and England."

Kings Named Louis

- King Louis XI of France was a great believer in astrology. Once he was so unnerved by an astrologer's correct prediction of a lady's death that he decided the astrologer should be killed, lest he divine royal secrets. He summoned the man to his chambers after instructing his servants to throw him out of a window to his death upon his signal. The king asked the astrologer if he could predict the day of his own death. The astrologer answered, "I shall die three days before you do, Your Majesty." The King decided not to have him thrown out the window after all.
- King Louis XIV required the assistance of over 100 people just to get ready in the morning.
- Louis XIV was boasting and bragging to his courtiers about how much power he had, saying that they were bound by law to do whatever he might tell them to do. The Comte de Guiche remarked that such absolute power must be accompanied by some reasonable restraint, but Louis responded, "If I commanded you to throw yourself into the sea, you would be the first to obey me." To his surprise, the count immediately got up and started walking quickly out of the room. The king asked where he was going, and the Count answered, "To learn to swim, Sire."
- Louis XIV loved to play billiards. After one shot a dispute arose, and the King asked nearby Comte de Gramont whether he thought the shot was legal or not. "You were in the wrong, Sire," said Gramont without hesitation. "How do you know? You didn't even see the shot!" exclaimed the King. Gramont replied, "If there had been the slightest doubt about the shot, the gentlemen who *did* see it would have all cried out that you were in the right."
- When Louis XIV was told that France's army was badly defeated at Blenheim, he cried out, "How could God do this to me after all I have done for Him?"
- Comte de Charolais, the cousin of Louis XIV, was very eccentric and not always in a nice way. He once shot a man who was working on the roof of a house just because he wanted to see him fall. The King pardoned his cousin of the crime, but added, "Let it be understood: I will similarly pardon anyone who shoots *you*."

Bits

- Emperor of Austria Francis Joseph heard of the reputation of comedian Girardi as a witty conversationalist. He invited the man to dinner, but was disappointed when the man only answered when spoken to and didn't have much to say. The

Emperor expressed disappointment, saying he had been looking forward to hearing Girardi's conversational gifts. Girardi replied, "Majesty, sometime you just try chatting with an emperor."

- Alexander Woollcott was a New York writer who contributed regularly to *The New Yorker*. While in London, he was invited to a dinner party with Prince Edward, who later became King Edward VIII. After eating, the guests were all assembled in a drawing room smoking and chatting when the Prince announced he would like to have a few words in private with Mr. Woollcott. As the people filed out of the room, Woollcott was envisioning announcement of some royal post or commission. Instead, Prince Edward said, "I understand that you have something to do with that magazine, *The New Yorker*." When Woollcott nodded, the Prince continued, "Then why the devil don't I get it more regularly? Do look into it, will you?" The party then resumed.

Kings Named George

- In 1917 King George V announced he was changing the royal surname from Saxe-Coburg-Gotha to the simple name Windsor. Kaiser Wilhelm of Germany heard the news and remarked that he couldn't wait to see the next performance of *The Merry Wives of Saxe-Coburg-Gotha*.

- King George II stopped at an inn where he was served an egg. The innkeeper charged an exorbitant price for the egg. The King commented, "Eggs must be very scarce around here." The innkeeper explained, "No sire, it is kings that are scarce."
- King George III was touring the royal stables when he asked a young stable hand how much he got paid. "They give me only my clothing and meals," answered the boy. "Be content," replied the King. "I have no more."
- King George III suffered from bouts of madness. During one such fit, he insisted on ending each and every sentence he spoke with the word "peacock."

—Rulers & Royalty— 147

His embarrassed ministers decided to at least minimize the damage by convincing the king that the word peacock was a very royal word which should therefore be whispered and not spoken aloud when he was speaking to his subjects. The suggestion was helpful.

* King George IV was, like his father, entirely looney. He had many strange delusions, which were powered by enormous amounts of cherry brandy. In particular, he believed he had commanded a gloriously victorious brigade at Waterloo. Sir William Knighton observed, "His Majesty has only to leave off cherry brandy, and, rest assured, he will gain no more victories." After reliving one imaginary battle, the king turned to the Duke of Wellington and asked, "Was it not so, duke?" The duke tactfully replied, "I have often heard Your Majesty say so."
* King George V was married to Queen Mary. The builders of a Cunard cruise liner were intending to name the ship the *RMS Queen Victoria*. But when they told King George they were going to name it "after the greatest queen in history," the King responded, "Oh, Mary will be *so* pleased!" The ship was named the *RMS Queen Mary* instead.

Rulers Named Charles

* Prince Charles was attending a show-business function when he was introduced to actress Susan Hampshire. She was wearing an extremely low-cut gown that left nothing to the imagination. Charles greeted her without flinching, saying, "Father told me that if I ever met a lady in a dress like yours, I must look her straight in the eyes."
* King Charles II, who ruled England in the 1600s, enjoyed telling stories of his life over and over again. Most of his attendants had heard the stories many times. The Earl of Rochester once observed that it was remarkable a man could remember so easily every detail of a story, and yet not remember he had told the same story to the same people the day before.
* When the explorer Hernando Cortéz returned home to make a report to King Charles V of Spain, he recommended that travel would be made much easier if a canal were dug across Panama. Charles rejected the suggestion, saying, "What God hath joined together let no man put asunder."
* Informed that his predecessor was dead and he was the new emperor of Austria, Charles I was stunned and emotional. "What should I do now?" he asked the bearer of the news. "I think the best thing is to order a new stamp to be made with my face on it."
* When Alexander I, Czar of Russia, was in Paris after Napoleon's defeat, he attended a fund-raising celebration at a local hospital. The plate was passed around for contributions, and an extremely pretty young girl was elected to take the collection plate to the Czar. He dropped in a handful of gold coins and said, "That's for your beautiful bright eyes." She thanked him, but immediately passed him the plate again. "What? More?" he asked. "Yes, sir," she said. "Now I want something for the poor."

Edwards

- As Queen Victoria lay dying, someone took the news to her son, Edward, Prince of Wales. "I wonder if she will be happy in heaven," he mused. "She will have to walk *behind* the angels— and she won't like that!"
- When the opera *The Wreckers* was first performed in 1909, King Edward VII was in attendance with his secretary. Conductor Sir Thomas Beecham later asked the secretary what the king had thought about the work. "I don't know," claimed the secretary. "Surely he must have made *some* comment to you during the performance," replied Beecham. "Well, yes," admitted the secretary. "He did say something. He suddenly woke up three-quarters of the way through and said, 'That's the fourth time that infernal noise has roused me!'"
- Edward VIII was visiting the U.S. and was enjoying an illegal drink in a speakeasy during Prohibition days when it was raided. Thinking quickly, the owners of the place hurried the King into the kitchen, put a chef's cap on his head, and told him to keep cooking eggs until the raid was over. The cops never recognized him.

Fast Facts

- British conductor Sir Thomas Beecham saw a woman on the street that he recognized, but he could not remember quite exactly who she was or how he knew her. He stopped to chat a bit with her, and remembered that she had a brother. Hoping for a clue to her identity, he asked how her brother was doing and whether he was still doing the same job. "Oh, he's fine," she answered, "and still King."
- Otto Bismarck was Chancellor to William the Emperor in the late 1800s. At a state dinner, a talkative American woman seated next to him addressed him properly as "Your Highness" during the first course. When the second course arrived, she was calling him "Mr. Chancellor" and by the time the third course arrived he had become "My dear Mr. Bismarck." When the fourth course arrived, he smiled and said, "My first name is Otto."
- Marie Therese Charlotte Angouleme, daughter of Marie Antoinette and Louis XVI, was a young child when she was playing with a maid. Taking the maid's hand in her own, she counted five fingers, then exclaimed, "What? You have five fingers, too, just like me!"
- John Baptiste Bernadotte was a French general who rose from humble origins to become king. Once when he fell ill the doctor insisted he must be bled. He steadfastly refused to let him do so. As his health continued to decline, he finally gave in to the physician and allowed himself to be bled. First, however, he exacted a promise from the doctor that he would keep secret what he found underneath the royal robes. There, tatooed on his forearm, were the words, "Death to all kings."

Elizabeths

- In 1956 Queen Elizabeth, wife of King Albert I, visited Warsaw. A chief of

protocol took her to mass. "Are you a Catholic?" she asked him. "Believing, but not practicing," he answered. "Are you a communist?" she asked. "Practicing, but not believing," he replied.
- Edward de Vee, Earl of Oxford, was bowing very, very low to Elizabeth I, Queen of England, when he farted quite loudly. He was so embarrassed that he spent the next several years traveling abroad. When he next saw the queen years later, her first words to him were "My lord, I had forgot the fart."
- Elizabeth I lived in obscurity while her half sister Mary reigned as Queen. During that time a knight was very rude to her. When Elizabeth took the throne after Mary, the same knight appeared on his knees before her, begging her forgiveness. She told him to get up and said, "Do you not know that we are descended of the lion, whose nature is not to prey upon the mouse or any other such small vermin?"
- Elizabeth II, who still reigns over the United Kingdom, was once in the Bahamas when her host used a pen from his pocket to stir her drink. "That's all right in our company, but what happens in high society?" the Queen asked.
- Queen Elizabeth and Prince Phillip were visiting President Ford at the White House. The President's son Jack was getting ready for a dinner party when he found he did not have any studs for his cuffs. He rushed to his father's room to borrow some. When he stepped into the elevator, he was alarmed to find it was already occupied by the Queen, the Prince, and his parents. Mrs. Ford was dismayed to have to introduce her half-dressed, unkempt son to the Queen, but the Queen took one look at the rumpled hair and the unbuttoned shirt and said, "I have one just like that!"
- Queen Mother Elizabeth, mother of the current Queen Elizabeth, was visiting Marshal Lyautey at Vincennes. During tea on the lakeshore, she said to him, "You are so powerful— would you do something for me?" He agreed. She asked him, "The sun is in my eyes— could you make it disappear?" Just then a cloud passed over the sun. The guests were amazed. Elizabeth thanked him. "I saw the cloud coming," she whispered to her neighbor.
- During the bombing raids of World War II, someone asked Queen Elizabeth whether she and her daughters, Elizabeth and Margaret Rose, would leave England for their safety. She insisted, "The children will not leave unless I do. I shall not leave unless their father does, and the King will not leave the country in any circumstances whatsoever."
- After a photography session, the photographer was showing Queen Elizabeth I the photos when he asked her if she would like him to retouch them to hide some wrinkles. She replied, "I would not want it to be thought that I had lived for all these years without having anything to show for it."

Queen Victoria

- Queen Victoria was on a ship crossing to Ireland when rough weather came up. A huge wave caused the ship to lurch violently, nearly knocking the queen to her feet. She told an attendant, "Go up to the bridge, give the admiral my

compliments, and tell him he's not to let that happen again."
- Queen Victoria received a letter from her grandson in which he asked her for an advance on his allowance. Instead of sending him money, she sent him a lengthy letter expounding upon the value of thrift and hard work. The grandson sold the letter for 25 pounds.
- After Queen Victoria died, her children visited her mausoleum every year on the anniversary of her death. Once a dove flew into the crypt, flying in circles inside. "It must be Mama's spirit!" they cried. "No, I am sure it's not," contradicted Princess Louise. "Yes, it must be Mama's spirit!" they protested. "No," said Louise, "I am sure dear Mama's spirit would never have ruined Beatrice's hat."

The Final Fact

Ferdinand I, Emperor of Austria in the 1800s, was insane. The most coherent sentence of his entire reign was, "I am the Emperor, and I want dumplings!"

SLEEP

The First Fact

In the U.S., more people visit their doctor for relief of insomnia than any other single complaint. Half the population suffers from insomnia at some point.

What A Tripp

In 1959 Peter Tripp, DJ for WMGM in New York, decided to raise money for the March of Dimes by performing a stunt. The stunt was to stay awake for 200 hours. He set up his recording booth in Times Square and came on the radio at hourly intervals to tell people how he was feeling, and he ran his usual evening show every night. The entire ordeal was watched by trained doctors and psychiatrists who were interested in seeing the effects of sleep deprivation. Tripp was never alone. Nurses were constantly checking his blood, urine, blood pressure, respiration, temperature, and brain waves. Tests tracked his muscular control, reaction time, memory, and psychological condition. Although his physical health did not change much, his psychological health deteriorated. On the third day he became disoriented. On the fourth day he began laughing at things no one else thought were funny. He was easily upset. He could not name common objects. Then hallucinations began. He screamed in horror when a doctor's tie seemed to turn into a live writhing snake. (Researchers now theorize that hallucinations resulting from sleep deprivation are actually waking dreams.) He was convinced the attendants were trying to slip drugs into his food to force him to sleep. Near the end he suffered from paranoia and was convinced the wake-a-thon was actually over but evil doctors were keeping him awake to torture him. Still, during his broadcasts for the first five days he continued his on-the-air patter without mishap, as if a reserved part of his brain kicked into action whenever he went on the air. After five and a half days, he became so incoherent that physicians put him on a stimulant. At this point his mental perception and alertness improved drastically. Tripp stayed awake for 201 hours, 10 minutes: eight days and nine hours. This set a world record. He slept for 13 hours afterwards and said he felt fine when he awoke. However, he complained that for the next several months he felt somewhat depressed.

Sleep Schedules

- Two experimenters in 1938 spent two months living in the darkness of Kentucky's Mammoth Cave. For the first month they lived 21-hour days using electric lights, and for the second month they lived 28-hour days. Although the men felt that they had adjusted to the new schedule, their bodies showed through blood and urine tests and temperature readings that they were still operating on a 24-hour cycle.
- People transferred to the perpetual night of the Arctic Circle tend to sleep about an hour longer each night.

- The accident rate in industry for night workers is almost twice the rate as those who work only in the day.
- A survey conducted by the Department of Transportation revealed that ten percent of all traffic accidents may be sleep related, and as many as 20% of all drivers have drifted off to sleep behind the wheel at some point.

Quote

"Frequent naps will keep you from getting old, especially if you take them while driving."
-Evan Esar

Universal Need

- Bats sleep longer than any other mammal: 20 out of every 24 hours. Lions sleep 17 hours out every 24. Squirrels and cats sleep about 14 hours a day; chimps about 11; donkeys only about 4. The sleep of moles is very like our sleep: it lasts 8 hours, with 2 hours spent dreaming. EEGs show the brain's electrical activity during the sleep of a mole is very much like ours. All birds sleep, and they all experience dreams as well, although they spend very little time dreaming. Zebra herds sleep in shifts, with half the herd sleeping while the other half stands guard. Horses can sleep lightly while standing; moderately if they have support for their head; but they must lie down to sleep heavily. They sleep on their sides 85% of the time, and on their stomachs 15% of the time.
- Ground squirrels hibernate every year for a certain period of time. Even if they are kept in warm, light rooms where there is plenty of food available, they will still hibernate for the usual period.
- Most plants show some primitive form of sleep. For instance, the sugar in an ear of ripened corn will flow downward through the stalk and into the roots at night. In the morning, the sugar rises again. That's why an ear of corn tastes starchy if picked in the evening, but sweet when picked in the morning.

Bedtime Stories

- William Johnson was the Administrator of American Indian Affairs. He had much influence over the Mohawks and Iroquios in the mid-1700s. Once a shipment of very expensive suits he had ordered arrived from England. The Mohawk chief admired the suits very much, and later told Johnson he had had a dream in which Johnson presented him with one of the suits. Johnson wanted to preserve good relations with the tribe, so he took the hint and gave the chief the finest suit. A little later Johnson told the chief he too had had a dream, in which the Mohawks had presented him with 5,000 acres of fertile land next to the Mohawk River. The chief gave the land to Johnson, remarking as he did, "I will dream no more with you. You dream too hard for me."

- Spencer Compton Cavendish Devonshire held many political appointments in Britain in the 1800s. In the middle of his very first speech in the House of Commons, he gave a great yawn. Disraeli remarked, "To anyone who can betray such languor in such circumstances, the highest posts should be open."
- Prince Albert, husband of Queen Victoria in the 1800s, was unable to stay awake late at night. At a concert at Buckingham Palace, he nodded off. Queen Victoria poked him awake, but soon he nodded off again. Several times this happened. The following day it was reported: "The Queen was charmed, and Albert looked beautiful, and slept quietly as usual."
- Carl Sandburg was invited to a dress rehearsal of a play in order to give his opinion of the production. He slept through most of the performance. The author complained, saying that he had really wanted Sandburg's opinion of the play. "Sleep *is* an opinion," he insisted.
- Alfred Hitchcock fell asleep at a party. After he had been sleeping for four hours, his wife woke him up and told him it was time to go home. "But it's hardly 1:00!" cried Hitchcock. "If we go home now, they'll think we aren't enjoying ourselves!"
- John Wesley, a British preacher after whom the Wesleyan Methodist Church is named, was giving a sermon one day when he noticed several people asleep. Suddenly he shouted out, "Fire! Fire!" They awoke with a start and wanted to know where the fire was. He replied, "In Hell, for those who sleep under the preaching of the word!"
- Jack Warner, founder of Warner Brothers, was in the habit of taking an afternoon nap in his office each day. There were strict orders that he not be disturbed. One day in the middle of his nap, Bette Davis blustered past the protesting secretary and burst in on Warner's nap. She began ranting and raving about a script she found unsuitable. Warner grabbed his phone and called his secretary. "Come in and wake me up! I'm having a nightmare!" he yelled. Bette Davis had to laugh, and the crisis was resolved in short order.
- Russian composer Anton Rubinstein would often sleep quite late, sometimes missing important appointments. In desperation, his wife devised a scheme certain to get him out of bed. She would go up to the piano above his bedroom and loudly play unresolved chords. Rubinstein couldn't stand unresolved chords and would jump up and rush to the piano to play the final notes. While he was thus occupied, his wife would sneak into his bedroom and make up the bed.

Fast Fact

In an experiment with sleep learning, a tape containing Russian words was played to subjects as soon as they entered deep sleep. Twelve Russian nouns were pronounced over and over again, with their English translations. Some subjects, upon waking in the morning, remembered as many as four of the words. They had better recall if the tape was played during a light period of sleep just before morning.

Tossing And Turning

One study on sleep incorporated rats and a large turning cylinder. The drum rotated slowly in a pool of water. The rats were easily able to walk in the direction opposite of the turning cylinder. If they stopped walking, they were dumped onto the water at the bottom. Food and water were readily available. The only problem the rats faced was the need to walk constantly. As soon as they fell asleep, the revolving drum plunged them into the water. Researchers found that young rats adapted very quickly and were able to survive for weeks at a time. They learned to sleep in twelve-second snatches, with twelve seconds being the time it took the turning drum to dump them into the water. They would awaken the moment before disaster, scurry to the top, then immediately doze off for another twelve-second nap. However, only young rats were able to adapt so well. Older rats could only stand the routine for a few days at a time.

Sleeping In

- In a sleep lab, volunteers who got eight hours of sound sleep were tested for reaction time on a number of different tasks. The following night they were shorted on their sleep. When the tests were repeated, it was not surprising that their marks fell as their reaction time increased. Following a normal eight hour sleep, reaction times returned to normal. The next night, they were allowed to sleep more than eight hours. Researchers were surprised to see that their reaction time increased after oversleeping just as it had when they underslept.
- A survey of 800,000 people showed that people who characteristically get ten hours of sleep suffered twice as many heart attacks and three and a half times as many strokes as people who slept seven hours or less.

Snoring

- There are over 300 patents on devices to prevent snoring.
- About 25% of people snore occasionally, and one out of eight is a chronic snorer. More men than women snore.
- The decibel level of some snorers has been registered at only one decibel lower than a jackhammer at a distance of ten feet.
- When Dear Abby ran a letter from a woman requesting help with her husband's snoring problem, Abby asked readers for advice. She was swamped with over 150,000 letters.
- Winston Churchill snored at the 35-decibel level, as measured by a naval officer on board a ship in August, 1944.

—Sleep—

- President Theodore Roosevelt once snored so loudly in the hospital that nearly every patient in the wing complained.
- Harry Christy of Lewiston, Idaho was elected Idaho's snoring champion in September 1944 at the Boise Veteran's Hospital. He won out over W.H. Gilman of Twin Falls, who had held the title for 17 years. Judges said Gilman's snoring had become "too jerky" to retain the title.

Nighty Night

- In July of 1968 a taxi driver in Bermuda fell asleep in the back of his cab in a parking lot. Someone stole his wallet, tie, and shirt while he slept.
- According to a Baltimore newspaper, a 300-pound cabbie went to sleep in his cab after working all night. He snored so loudly he attracted a crowd. A cop tried to wake him to no avail. By the time he awakened, there were reportedly several hundred people watching him snore.
- On July 12, 1966 a burglar in Sao Paulo, Brazil, fell asleep in the house of Mr. Reutera. When the owner of the house returned home, he heard snoring in the bedroom. When the burglar awakened, he was facing an angry homeowner and the police.
- Travis Zellis was in jail in Cincinnati, serving a 90-day sentence for stealing an amplifier from a nightclub. Soon after his imprisonment, jailers began receiving complaints from other prisoners who couldn't sleep at night due to his profound snoring. Zellis was released early so the other prisoners could get some sleep.

The Final Fact

The most expensive bed (and the most comfortable) is one made of a foot-thick layer of small ceramic beads. When compressed air is pumped into the bed, the beads float on air, creating an incredibly soft cushion that offers almost no resistance to the body. The beds are made for burn patients. Waterbeds were invented by hospitals to help prevent bedsores.

Index

A

Aaron, Hank 26
Abbot & Costello 75, 109
Academy Award 78
Acrobat 9
Adams, John 121
Aga Khan 70
Agate 72
Age 103, 108, 121, 132, 135, 149, 154
AIDS 100
Air pollution 5
Airplane 86, 97, 116, 118, 120, 137, 138
Airport 6, 7
Alaska 3, 83
Albert, Prince 153
Alcohol 82, 141, 148, 149. *See also* Drunk Driving
Ali, Muhammed 65
Allen, Gracie 97
Alligator 18
Aluminum 1
Alzheimer's disease 104
Amethyst 72
Amish 92
Ant 19–24
Antibiotic 49, 144
Antietam 119
Antiseptic 127
Antoinette, Marie 148
Ape 134
Aphid 19
Appendix 66
Appert, Nicholas 56
Aquamarine 71
Arctic Circle 152
Aristotle 10, 117
Armored car 13
Art 99, 134
Arthur, Chester 122
Asche, Oscar 65
ASPCA 10, 76
Aspirin 82
Astaire, Fred 65, 74, 75
Aster, John Jacob 31
Astrologer 134
Astronaut 61, 82, 84, 134
Astronomer 134
Atomic bomb 118
Auto accident 2, 3, 4, 5
Autograph 125
Avon 133

B

Baboon 99
Baby 15, 45, 103, 105, 127, 132, 135
Ball, Lucille 75, 96, 105
Ballet 7
Balzac, Honoré 138
Bank 46, 101
Barbie 138
Barkley, Alben 55, 95
Barrymore, Ethyl 106
Barrymore, John 106
Barrymore, Maurice 73
Baseball 25–30, 79, 108, 135
Baskin-Robbins 87
Bat (animal) 152
Bathroom 31, 123
Baugh, Laura 65
Bayonet 56
Beard 126, 133, 134
Beatty, Warren 75
Bed 155
Bedbug 117
Bee 80
Beecham, Thomas 109, 148

— Index —

Beer 77
Beethoven 93
Beetle 49
Ben Hur 75
Benchley, Peter 73
Benchley, Robert 110
Benny, Jack 31
Bergen, Edgar 78, 109
Beriberi 141
Bernhardt, Sarah 108
Berra, Yogi 27
Berry 48
Bible 41
Bird 152
Birds, The 77
Birdseye, Clarence 60
Blair, Linda 75
Blanc, Mel 75
Blondin, Charles 9
Blood poisoning 131
Bolivia 136
Bolt, Tommy 65
Bomb 78, 120
Bond, James 64
Book 84, 135
Boone, Daniel 95
Borge, Victor 114
Boxing 124
Brady, Jim 67
Brahms 93
Brain 104, 105, 152. *See also* Memory
Bread 59, 90, 139
Brice, Fanny 109
Broccoli 46
Brooks, Mel 73
Bubonic Plague 129
Buchanan, James 122
Burns, George 97, 108
Burton, Richard 68, 75
Butler 17
Button 118

C

Cadillac 46

Calcium 142
Calendar 43
California 1, 3, 5, 135
Cancer 80, 132
Cannon 119
Cantor, Eddie 86
Captain Calculus 5
Car 1–6, 16, 18, 32, 46, 125
Carmichael, Hoagy 61
Carotene 143
Carpet 44
Carrot 143
Carson, Johnny 114
Carter, Garnet 64
Carter, Jimmy 126
Cartoon 15
Caruso, Enrico 7
Casablanca 77
Castro, Fidel 89
Cat 116, 125, 152
Cato 106
Cattle 17
Cave 38, 152
Cavities 135. *See also* Teeth
Celery 81
Celler, Emanuel 107
Cello 8
Cement 1
Cemetery 36, 41, 73, 78, 83, 107. *See also* Death
Censorship 77
Central Park 84
Chair 79
Chaplin, Charlie 74, 95
Charisse, Cyd 96
Charlemagne 71
Charles, King 85, 147
Charles, Prince 147
Cheese 119, 130
Chevalier 106
Chicago 6
Chicken 5, 43, 45, 79, 100, 103, 141
Chicken poop 5
Child support 137
Chimpanzee 98, 103, 152
China 1, 137

— Index —

Chocolate 88
Chopin 93
Christmas 133
Churchill, Winston 93, 106, 108, 154
Cigar 123
Cinnamon 81
Circus 9
Clement, Pope 71
Cleveland, Grover 84, 122
Clinton, George 83
Clock 93
Clover 90
Cobb, Ty 29
Coca-Cola 109, 137
Cocaine 136
Cochrane, Josephine 58
Coffin 136
Coin 33, 126
Colbert, Claudette 77
Collagen 142
Common cold 106
Coney Island 127
Confucious 93
Conners, Chuck 29
Conscious fund 133
Convenience store 134
Cookie 59, 60, 126
Coolidge, Calvin 124
Cork 57
Corn 152
Cortéz, Hernando 147
Costello, Lou 75
Couch 110
Counterfeit money 35
Crane, Ichabod 95
Crawford, Joan 96
Credit card 34
Crime 13, 39, 124, 136, 137, 155
Crocker, Betty 109
Crocker, Sewall 2
Crockett, Davy 95
Crow 64
Cryogenic 134
Cullinan (diamond) 69
Curie, Madame 94
Czar 147

D

Dali, Salvador 134
Dance 7, 74
Davis, Bette 153
Dear Abby 154
Death 81, 84, 97, 105, 124, 127, 132, 136, 145, 148. *See also* Cemetery, Ghost, Suicide, Will
Death row 137
DeBeers Mining 69
Defector 136
Dehumidifier 16
De'Medici, Catherine 85
Diabetic 82
Diamond 67–72
Dice 45
Diet 42, 109, 132, 141, 143. *See also* Food
Dietrich, Marlene 75
Dinner party 146
Dinosaur 103
Dishwasher 58
Disney, Walt 78
Divorce 13, 137. *See also* Wedding, Marriage
Doctor 15. *See also* Medicine
Dr. Jekyll & Mr. Hyde 37
Dog 25, 83, 103, 109, 125
Doll 138
Donkey 152
Douglas, Kirk 96
Dove 150
Draft resister 135
Dream 37, 38, 39, 41, 112, 153
Drug addiction 82
Drunk driving 2, 3
Duel 121
Dumas, Alexandre 107
Dumplings 150
DuPont 1, 56
Durante, Jimmy 75, 114
Durocher, Leo 27
Dvorak 93
Dynamite 16
Dysart, Willis 138

— Index —

Dyslexia 82

E

Ear 105
Earthquake 100, 135
Echo 101
Eck, Johnny 9
Education 116
Edward, King 148
Edward, Prince 146
Egg 139, 143, 146, 148
Eisenhower, Dwight 65
Election 93, 111, 123, 138
Electric 135
Elephant 98, 103, 114
Elizabeth, Queen 36, 149
Ellery Queen 93
Emperor 147, 148, 150
Eskimo Pie 88
Estrogen 117
Execution 137
Eye 80, 81, 82, 104, 124

F

Faces 138
Farmer, Fannie 55
Farragut, David 115
Fart 149
Fax 16
Ferdinand I 150
Fever 83
Fields, W.C. 77
Fillmore, Millard 121
Fire 123
Firemen 17
Firestone Tires 3
First Lady 84, 124
Fish 60, 80, 140
Fishing 14
Fitzgerald, F. Scott 73
Fleming, Alexander 27, 130
Florida 142
Flower 46, 47, 102. *See also* Plant
Fluoridation 138
Fly 131
Flynn, Errol 75
Flynn, Sean 75
Food 11, 55, 56, 59, 60, 64, 81, 85, 90, 109, 133, 139. *See also* Diet
Football 79
Ford cars 1
Ford, Gerald 42, 65, 149
Ford, Henry 1
Fothergill, Bob 27
Fox 100
Frankenstein 73
Franklin, Benjamin 108
Freelance 45
French Connection 75
Frisch, Frankie 26
Frog 49–54
Frosted Flakes 59
Fruit cake 120
Fungus 19

G

Gable, Clark 75, 78
Gabor, Zsa Zsa 96
Gambling 13, 79. *See also* Dice
Garfield, James 122
Garland, Judy 73
Garlic 48
Garnet 72
Gasoline 3, 5, 97. *See also* Petroleum, Car, Oil
Gehrig, Lou 27
General Mills 59
General Motors 3
George, King 146, 147
Georgia 83
Germs 127
Getty, J. Paul 31
Gettysburg 122
Ghost 11, 83
God 16, 17, 32
Goethe 108
Gold 31
Golf 26, 61–66, 79
Gomez, Lefty 26
Gone With the Wind 76

Good Humor 88
Gooden, Dwight 26
Gopher 152
Grable, Betty 75
Grant, Cary 108, 127
Grant, Ulysses S. 122
Grass 98
Gregory, Dick 92
Grey, Zane 101
Guava 142
Gun 13, 14, 37, 118, 121, 136, 145
Gymnastics 79

H

Hagen, Walter 65
Haig, Alexander 120
Hair 126, 133. *See also* Beard, Mustache
Halibut 140
Hallucination 49, 82, 151
Hamilton, Alexander 84
Hamilton, Margaret 73
Hammerstein, Oscar 9
Hangover 82. *See also* Alcohol
Hardy, Oliver 74
Harlow, Jean 78
Harrison, Benjamin 123
Harrison, William Henry 123
Harvard 27
Hawaii 129
Head-up displays 16
Hearing 105
Heart 45, 104, 134
Hepburn, Katharine 78
Herbs 48. *See also* Garlic, Plant
Hieroglyph 38
High blood pressure 104
High Jinks 44
Hijacking 137
Hine, Jimmy 61
Hines, Duncan 55
Hippocrates 85
Hippopotami 75
Hitchcock, Alfred 77, 153
Hitler, Adolph 93, 117, 118

Hoax 68, 110
Holiday 133
Hollywood 29, 73, 74, 76, 78, 127
Homeless 137
Homework 135
Honey 116. *See also* Bee
Hoover, Herbert 125
Hope, Bob 75, 106, 109
Horse 7, 10, 14, 43, 81, 98, 103, 113, 117, 152
Hospital 127. *See also* Medicine
Howarth, Donald 11
Howe, Elias 37
Howe, Gordie 65
Hudson, Rock 75
Hum 135
Human calculator 138
Hunting 14, 109, 111

I

IBM 6
Ibogaine 82
Ice 9, 85, 98, 111, 136
Ice cream 85
Immigrant 84
Import 135
In vitreo 81
Incubator 127
Indian 129, 141, 152
Infection 127
Infidelity 134
Insanity 146, 147, 150. *See also* Hallucination
Insect 141. *See also* specific name
Insomnia 151
Insulin 81
Insurance 3, 109, 134, 135
Inventor 37, 56, 57, 58, 87
Iowa 6, 14
Irving, Washington 95

J

Jackson, Andrew 121
Jackson, Michael 138
Jackson, Nelson 2

— Index —

Jail 137, 155
Japan 17, 65, 77, 84, 118, 135
Jasper (gem) 72
Jaws (movie) 73
Jaywalking 137
Jeep 6
Jefferson, Thomas 121
Jell-O 76
Jeritz, Maria 7
Jewel 67–72
Jewelry 31
Job 137, 138. *See also* Unemployment
Jogging 104
John (name) 92
Johnson, Louisa 84
Johnson, Lyndon B. 125
Johnson, Nancy 85
Jones, John Paul 115
Journal of Irreproducible Results 17

K

Karloff, Boris 73, 75, 96
Kennedy, J. F. 32
Kennedy, John 93
Kerosene 11
Kerr, Jean 110
Kidnap 13
King 148
King Kong 76
King Lear 11
Kings 145–150
Kipling, Rudyard 40
Kitchen 55–60
Kitchenmaid 58
Knife 10, 14, 59
Knight 45
Kohinoor Diamond 69
Krill 83
Kuwait 40

L

Labrador retrievers 13
Language 43–48. *See also* Word origin

Lard 117
Laughter 15, 109
Laurel, Stan 74
Lawyer 137
Lead (metal) 5, 37
Leeuwenhoek, Anthony van 128
Lemon 141
Liberace 96
Library 97
Life expectency 103
Lightbulb 6
Lime 141
Limousine 5
Lincoln, Abe 33, 119, 122
Linoleum 58
Lion 152
Lister, Joseph 127
Liver 140, 144
Lizard 80
Lloyd, Harold 78
Lockheed 95, 120
L.A. 6, 137
Lotito, Michel 8
Louis, King 145
Louis XI 8
Lugosi, Bela 73, 75
Lung 128

M

Mac Truck 3
MacArthur, Charles 74
Macbeth 11
MacLaine, Shirley 75
Magazine 146
Maggot 128
Magic 9, 10
Magruder, Lloyd 39
Mail 92, 100, 122, 133, 147
Malaria 82, 130
Malnutrition 137
Mammoth Cave 152
Manhattan 5
Mankiewicz, Joseph 73
Maranville, Rabbit 25, 26
Marriage 107, 122, 134. *See also* Wedding, Divorce

Marx, Groucho 95
Marx, Harpo 67, 96
Marx, Zeppo 101
Mary, Queen 147
Maryland 24
Maugham, W. Somerset 107
Mayflower 91
McCarthy, Charlie 78
McCollum, Elmer 139
McKinley, William 123
Measurement 55, 138
Medicare 134
Medicine 127, 128, 129, 131, 132, 134, 139, 148
Melba, Nellie 90
Memory 80, 105, 107, 147, 148. *See also* Brain
Merman, Ethel 109
Message in a bottle 133
Message to God 16
Meter 138
Methane 5
Michelangelo 108
Microscope 128
Midge 83
Milk 77, 86, 89, 143
Miniature golf 64
Minimum wage 137
Minneapolis 133
Minnelli, Liza 73
Mint 48
Missing children 136
Mr. Eat-All 8
MIT 80
Mitterand, Francois 70
Mix, Tom 77
Mobile home 135
Model T 1
Modelling 138
Mohawk 153
Mold 130
Mole 152
Monaco 84
Money 31, 32, 33, 35. *See also* Coin, Bank, Counterfeit
Monkey 37, 81

Monteax, Pierre 107
Moon 84
Morgan, J.P. 34
Morris, Desmond 134
Moses, Grandma 108
Mosquito 130
Moth 102
Mother's Day 133
Mouse 84, 103
Movie 2, 75, 86, 97, 101, 138. *See also* Hollywood
Moyers, Bill 125
Mud 26
Muir, John 33
Muscle 104
Music 8, 10, 81, 91, 93, 109, 114, 133, 153
Musical saw 75
Mustache 134
Mustard 44

N

Name 91–96, 122, 125, 148
Nanny 17
Napoleon 56
NASA 67
National City Lines 3
National Geographic 17
Nauseau 134
Nelson, Christian 87
Netherlands 98
New York City 1, 5, 6, 84, 92, 133, 136, 137
New Yorker (Magazine) 146
Newman, Paul 78
Newsom, Bobo 25
Niacin 143
Niagara Falls 9, 136
Nicaragua 138
Nicklaus, Jack 26
Nimoy, Leonard 101
Niven, David 77
Nixon, Richard 30, 126
Nobel, Alfred 16
Nobel, Ignatius 17
Nose 75

Nuclear weapon 135
Nylon 80

O

Ocean 83
Odor Orchestra 9
Office chair 79
Oil 40, 84. *See also* Gasoline, Petroleum
Olives 33
Olympics 63
O'Neal, Tatum 78
Opera 7, 90, 113, 148
Orange juice 82
Oranges 142
Orangutan 98
Oreo 59
Oscar Award 78
Ostrich 99
Othello 11
Ott, Mel 27

P

Paige, Leroy 108
Paint 2, 113
Panama Canal 147
Paper Moon 78
Paper towel 57
Paré, Amboise 127
Paris 13
Park, Roy 55
Parker, Dorothy 111
Parkinson's disease 49
Parrhasius 100
Parrot 9
Pasteur, Louis 127
Patent 85, 87
Peacock 146
Pearl 71
Pellagra 143
Pencil 131
Penicillin 27, 81, 130
Pepsi 138
Perceval, Spencer 38
Perot, Ross 36

Pet 81, 121. *See also* Cat, Dog
Petroleum 1, 116
Phillip, Prince 107, 149
Phillips Petroleum 3
Phlegm 47
Photograph 106, 149
Piano 7, 8, 91, 114, 153
Picasso, Pablo 108
Pictograph 38
Pig 8, 9, 89
Pigeon 103
Ping-pong 79
Pitt, Thomas 69
Plants 47, 83, 98, 152. *See also* Flower
Plastination 16
Plunkett, Roy 56
Pogo 115
Poison 50
Poisoned arrow 50
Police 6, 136, 137. *See also* Crime
Polio 125
Polk, James 122
Pollution 54. *See also* Air Pollution
Polo 79
Ponce de Leon 142
Pontiac 5
Pool (billiards) 121
Pope Clement 71
Pope John Paul II 10
Popeye 144
Population 83
Potato 142
Poverty 137
Practical joke 110
Pregnancy 135
Presidents 83, 91, 121–126. *See also* specific name
Presley, Elvis 133
Prohibition 148
Psychic 145
Pujol, Joseph 12
Push-ups 79
Pygmy 99

Index

Q

Quarantine 129
Quartz 71, 72
Quayle, Dan 66
Queen 145, 148–150
Quinine 130

R

Radiation 118
Radish 46
Railroad 6
Rain 83
Rat 109, 139, 154
Reading 135
Reagan, Ronald 126, 134
Real estate 135
Recycle 79
Redford, Robert 75
Refrigerator 138
Reindeer 45
Religion 149, 153
Restaurant 18, 34, 55
Resumé 135
Retirement 132
Reuben, David 88
Revere, Paul 93
Reykjavik, Iceland 17
Rhode Island 3
Rhodes, Cecil 69
Rhodesia 69
Riot 89
Roach 99
Robot 84
Rockefeller, John D. 35
Rogers, Ginger 74, 96
Rogers, Will 78
Rollerskating 7
Roosevelt, Franklin 86, 125
Roosevelt, Theodore 14, 123, 155
Rossini 33
Rothschild, Nathan 35
Roxy Theater 77
Rubble, Betty 139
Rubinstein, Anton 153
Rubinstein, Arthur 108
Ruby 68, 72
Rum 142
Rumor 117
Russell, Lillian 67
Russell Stover Candy 88
Ruth, Babe 5, 125

S

Salt 83
Sandburg, Carl 153
Sapphire 68, 70, 72
Sarazen, Gene 65
Schubert 93
Schumann 93
Scotland Yard 13
Scott, Clarance 57
Scurvy 139, 141, 142
Seatbelt 4
Secret Service 35
Secretary 43
Semmelweis 131
Sepoy Rebellion 117
Sewing machine 37, 133
Sex 144
Sex change 134
Shakespeare 11, 91
Shark 73
Shaw, George Bernard 108
Shea Stadium 135
Shephard, Alan 61
Sheridan, Richard 112
Ship 98, 113, 115, 119, 129, 147, 149
Shirt 44, 80
Shoe 79, 133, 135
Shrapnel, Henry 120
Silkworm 83
Skin 142
Sleep 37, 105, 123, 151–155
Sleepeaters 42
Sleepwalkers 42
Smallpox 129
Smith (name) 92
Smokers 40
Smoking 123
Snake 49
Snead, Sam 61, 66

Snoring 154, 155
Snow 85
Snow White 78
Soap 18
Sober Sue 9
Social Security 92, 133
Soda 87. *See also* Coca-Cola
South Africa 11
Spam 59
Speech 109, 121, 125
Spelling 136
Spielberg, Steven 73
Spinach 144
Spitball 28
Spitting 79
Sportsman Memorials 14
Spy 117
Squirrel 152
Stage coach 14
Stamps 122, 147
Standard Oil 3
Statue 33
Stealth Bomber 116
Steel 1
Stengel, Casey 25, 107
Stethoscope 128
Stevenson, Robert Louis 37
Stock market 36
Strawberry 48
Streaking 17
Street 135
Striptease 113
Submarine 17
Sugar 89
Suicide 99, 105, 122
Suit 153
Sundae 88
Swim 79, 145
Sword Swallowers 10
Sybaris 10

T

Taft, William Howard 124
Tarzan 76
Taste bud 82
Tatoo 148
Tax 3, 46, 133
Taylor, Elizabeth 68, 75
Teeth 81, 97, 98, 135. *See also* Toothbrush
Teflon 56–57
Telephone 18, 35, 133
Temple, Shirley 73
Ten Commandments 76
Tennis 79
Termite 24, 64
Texas 3, 5, 15
Thales 33
Thurber, James 105
Time 84
Titanic 40
Toad 49, 52, 53. *See also* Frog
Toilet 118
Toll House cookie 60
Tolstoy, Leo 108
Toothbrush 32
Train 2, 53, 59, 72
Travino, Lee 79
Truman, Harry 95, 120, 125
Tschaikovsky 93
Tuberculosis 128
Tupper, Earl S. 56
Tupperware 56
Turban 69
Turquoise 71
TV 7, 16, 59, 75, 126, 137
TV dinner 59
Twain, Mark 51, 106
Twins 91, 92
Tyler, John 122
Typographical errors 111

U

Ultrasound 80
Ultraviolet radiation 80
Umbrella 10, 133
Umpire 26, 27
Unemployment 138
United Nations 17

— Index —

V

Vaccine 80, 121, 129
Venus 67
Verdi 93
Victoria, Queen 148, 149, 153
Vitamin 139–144
Volcano 100
Vulture 80

W

Waddell, Rube 26
Wailing Wall 16
Wakefield, Ruth 60
Walk 83
Walking upright 15
Walton, Frederick 57
Wampum 35
War 43, 86, 98, 115–120, 128, 130, 133
War and Peace (book) 76
Warner, Jack 153
Washington D.C. 132
Washington, George 85, 121, 129
Water 16, 52, 138, 154
Waterbed 155
Watergate 97
Watt, James 37
Wedding 75, 85, 99, 107, 122, 124, 134. *See also* Marriage
Weed 48
Weissmuller, Johnny 76
Welles, Orson 11
Wesley, John 153
Whale 83
Whistle 135
White House 121
Will 40, 97, 133. *See also* Death
Wilson, Edith 124
Wilson, Woodrow 109, 124
Wine 56, 117, 128
Witch 44
Wizard of Oz 73
Wood, Nicholas 11
Woollcott, Alexander 32, 146

Word origin 14, 28, 33, 43, 44, 45, 47, 48, 50, 55, 58, 71, 79, 90, 115, 127–132
World's Fair 87
Wray, Fay 76
Wrestling 79
Wristwatch 101, 111

Y

Yawn 18, 153
Yellow fever 130
Yoga 83
Young, William 85
Youngman, Henny 136
You're kidding 14

Z

'Z' 97
Zambia 100
Zappa, Frank 101
Zarb, Frank 97
Zebra 152
Zeno 97
Zeus 101
Ziegfeld, Florenze 97
Ziegler, Ron 97
Zink, M. 97
Zinnia 102
ZIP code 100
Zipper 101
Zoo 99, 134
Zorilla 97
Zoysia 98
Zucchini 100
Zuider Zee 98
Zulus 119
Zyzzyx 102

About the Author

J. Spencer completes most of her writing on a forest fire lookout tower in Montana. Any spare time is devoted to flower gardening, cowboy poetry, barbershop singing, nature photography, camping, and canoeing. Family consists of a crippled dog, an elderly cat, and a long-suffering spouse.

About the Cartoonist

Now 35, Moravek broke into cartooning seven years ago to spice up the procedure schedule of a southern Kansas City hospital's gastroenterology lab. Declared everything from 'evidence of an ailing mind' to 'sheer genius,' his *Gutz* cartoons successfully gleaned humor from a highly sensitive, bizarre subject without once resorting to a cheap shot. Selected *Gutz* cartoons still hang in a prominent physician's prep room.

Migration to the Great West brought Moravek into collusion with Helena, Montana's *Tidbits*. His weekly *Tardigrade Talons* cartoon strip enlivend the paper for many years.

Moravek currently works as the resident Radar O'Reilly in a local emergency room and intensive care, irritating staff and patients alike with righteous obsessive satire when not spending far too much time placating a pair of obnoxious cats at home.

Yes! *I'm interested in hearing about new Tidbits titles as they come available. Please put me on your mailing list!*

Name _____

Address _____

_____

City/State/Zip _____

Phone _____

Send to: Jes Press • P. O. Box 380 • Helena, MT 59624
1-800-6TIDBIT (1-800-684-3248)
Or see your local Tidbits distributor